I Like It Better
When You're Funny

CHARLES GRODIN

I Like It Better When You're Funny

WORKING IN TELEVISION
AND OTHER PRECARIOUS ADVENTURES

RANDOM HOUSE · NEW YORK

Library of Congress Cataloging-in-Publication Data

Grodin, Charles.
   I like it better when you're funny : working in television and other
precarious adventures / Charles Grodin.—1st ed.
      p. cm.
   ISBN 0-375-50784-1 (alk. paper)
   1. Grodin, Charles. 2. Motion picture actors and actresses—United
States—Biography. 3. Television personalities—United States—Biography. I. Title.

PN2287.G74 A3 2002
791.43′028′092—dc21
   [B]   2001048985

Printed in the United States of America on acid-free paper

98765432

First Edition

Book design by Mercedes Everett

To my brother, Jack. I've never had a bigger supporter.

Preface

"I like it better when you're funny." I've heard that said many times over the years, as I went from being a comedy actor in the movies to an often serious commentator on television.

Once I had a meeting with a fellow who was interested in my doing a syndicated show, who said, "You should be more like Regis."

When I was interviewed by a lady from *The New York Times,* before I began as a commentator for *60 Minutes II,* she asked in her article, "Is there anything more disappointing than a comic actor who decides to get serious? It's like hoping for a chocolate soufflé and getting spinach."

When I began to do an hour show on CNBC following Geraldo Rivera, the intention was for me to be the "dessert."

This is the story of how, after a few months, that changed. I then began a journey in television that was like nothing I ever imagined, engendering reactions that ranged from "You have become the conscience of America" to "How did that communist ever get his own talk show in the first place?"

Contents

I Like It Better
When You're Funny

A Horse Who Can Type

In the early 1970s, after two brief appearances with Johnny Carson on *The Tonight Show*, I was asked if I'd like to be under exclusive contract to Johnny as a late night talk-show guest. I was startled, recovered quickly, and said yes. I was told it had been done twice before, with David Steinberg and Joan Rivers.

I thought about what I might have done with Johnny Carson that would have made him want to put me under contract.

I specifically remember one question and answer. The movie *The Heartbreak Kid*, where I had my first starring role, had just opened. Johnny asked me what my family had thought of me in the picture. I said they hadn't seen it yet. They were waiting for it to open in the neighborhood theaters. That really made him laugh. It wasn't all that funny, but Johnny seemed to respond to the "sincerity" with which I said it.

That "sincerity," of course, was exactly the kind of thing that would later get me into difficulty. Actually it still does.

Over the years I watched several of Johnny's guests—David Letterman, Jay Leno, David Steinberg, and Joan Rivers, among others—be invited to that next exalted level of guest host. In a twenty-year period of appearing with Johnny, I wondered from time to time if that invitation would ever come for me.

One day after an appearance, I was standing in the hall with the talent coordinator, Bob Dolce, an unusually intense fella, who was always championing me on the show, as well as trying to shepherd me through its minefields. Bob would offer advice like "Let Johnny speak first," which I often didn't do, because that kind of minute planning could make you self-conscious. Bob said to me more than once, "I have no idea who you are once you're out there." I didn't know if he meant that as a compliment or a criticism, and I decided not to ask.

One day I was with Bob when the executive producer, the legendary Freddie De Cordova, approached. Freddie defined *smooth*. "Why shouldn't Charles Grodin be a guest host on *The Tonight Show*?" he thundered. "I always wondered about that myself," I said. Everyone chuckled, but not another word was ever said about it. Not that it was the most pressing question in my life, but I was curious. Why not? When I later asked Bob why the call never came, the answer was, "The unexpected thing they like about you as a guest might make America uncomfortable with you as a host."

It's not that easy to make America uncomfortable, but I had evidently succeeded to an alarming degree. I had even made my friends uncomfortable when they watched me on the show. They would tell me they'd leave the room when I came on, or stay and watch peeking through their fingers. What was I doing to cause such discomfort? I was kidding around. The problem was that only Johnny and a minority of viewers seemed to know it. So when

Johnny would ask, "How are you?" and I would refuse to answer, because I said I didn't believe it mattered to him how I felt—millions shuddered at the rudeness of it all. Plenty laughed, but more shuddered. Sometimes the audience would hiss, and Johnny would try to pacify them by holding up a hand and saying, "It's all right, I'm used to it."

Since being the host of a television show didn't rank in my top ten goals in life at that time, I didn't give a lot of thought to not being asked to guest host and continued on my merry way as an annoying guest. It's not that I'd wake up on the morning of an appearance and decide to be annoying. It's just that I didn't have a lot of faith in the alternative: "I'm very excited about my new movie." "She was a joy to work with." Right beneath all that, "Who cares?" screamed back at me. On the other hand, if I walked off the set, as I once did on *The Tonight Show*, saying, "The unfunny environment that preceded me out here makes it impossible to get laughs," at least it wasn't boring.

Actually, after that appearance I was told that Freddie De Cordova had said, "We won't be seeing Mr. Grodin for a while." I earlier wrote that after being under contract, I was regularly banned, not from the show but from appearing with Johnny. Guest hosts could still book me, and they did. I particularly remember being with Bill Cosby, because of what happened.

I was on for two segments. In the first, Bill got into a riff about my shoes. I don't remember anything weird about them, but of course, Bill can do a number on anything.

During the break, Freddie De Cordova came over to Bill and said, "Ask him a question. He'll know what to do." The Coz shot

Freddie a look I won't forget. The atmosphere was such that about halfway through the second segment, I was wishing Bill would go back to the shoe riff.

Years later, when I had dinner with Johnny, he told me he'd read that I said he had banned me from appearing with him, and he absolutely denied it. He went on to say that a number of things had been done in his name over the years he only later became aware of, my being banned among them.

Personally, I believe anything Johnny tells me, because he has never been shy about letting me know what he thinks. Once, when he knew he wasn't on camera, he shot me a look that made Cosby's look to Freddie De Cordova seem like a smile.

In any case, I never became a guest host on *The Tonight Show*.

It was in the early 1980s, while I was no longer exclusive to Johnny but still regularly appearing on *The Tonight Show,* that I also began to appear on *The Tomorrow Show,* hosted by Tom Snyder. One week, Tom was going to Egypt to interview Anwar Sadat and someone said, "Why not have Charles Grodin guest host?"

This time the offer came to host the show for a week. I immediately began to think of whom I would book for guests. My first thought was my friend Nick Arnold. I knew no one had ever heard of him, but he was about the wittiest person I'd ever met. He was a highly successful producer/director of television comedy and also as smart as they come. There was a catch. He had cerebral palsy and was not going to give any elocution lessons. In fact, it might be fair to say that a portion of the audience might not be able to understand what he was saying. Those who could would be repeating his lines the next day. When I suggested him as a guest, there was a long silence on the other end of the phone. A day later, I got a somewhat angry message that if I didn't sign my contract immediately, "We're going to get Kelly Lange!" Kelly was, and is at this writing, a newswoman from L.A. who definitely wasn't going to book someone with palsy who might not be comprehensible. I quickly said, "Contract? What contract?" (I hadn't even seen one.) Guesting or hosting a TV show always seemed like a party invite to me. Anyway, I immediately signed something, and the show went on. Nick Arnold was brilliant. The commentator I. F. Stone was pithy, and the surprise appearance of the week was Tom Snyder himself, who is as uncomfortable as a guest as he is marvelously at home as a host. It turned out that the Anwar Sadat interview had fallen through, and Tom was available to host after all, but he generously said that since they already had gotten me, go ahead and let me do it. That was the first of many kindnesses Tom Snyder bestowed on me over the years.

There was an extra value to all of this that I didn't know at the time. The executive producer of *The Tomorrow Show* was a man by the name of Roger Ailes, and it was he, almost fifteen years later, who would play a key role in my finally emerging as a talk show host.

It was around ten years later, in the early 1990s, when I began to think about hosting a talk show again. It wasn't a career move. In fact, it would have to be considered an anticareer move. I had made the movie *Midnight Run* and the *Beethoven* movies and was in the best position I'd ever been in in the film world, but I also had a young son, and I was often on the road. In *Midnight Run,* there were about fifteen different locations, including New Zealand. My family was almost always with me, but my wife and I felt that when our boy entered school, something had to change. He couldn't be constantly uprooted, and I had no intention of not being there regularly as a dad. That meant working in New York.

Only two options seemed possible—doing a television series or a talk show. For me, the choice was simple. With all due respect to the plus sides of a television series, it was the talk show that held out something unique to me. The reason for this was very simple. I would, if given a choice, rather speak in my own voice with my own words than in the voice of a fictional character saying lines from a script. With all the talk show guest appearances I had done over the previous twenty years or so, that too was almost always a fictional character. Here, really for the first time, that would not be the case.

Unknown even to the people who were considering hiring me, I've always had strong feelings about a lot of things without really having a venue where it would have been appropriate to express them.

As far as the audience is concerned, when I'm approached by people in public settings, about half of them cite work I've done as a character in movies, and half talk about what I've done as myself on television.

I appreciate all of it, but there's no question the comments on my television work resonate more, because it feels more personal.

There's a complicating issue to the movie feedback. It doesn't really feel appropriate to tell someone who's complimenting some movie I did that I might have liked it less than they did.

The Heartbreak Kid comes to mind. I thought it was a brilliant movie. However, I find my character, a young man who leaves his wife on his honeymoon, more frightening than funny. Of course, in fairness, some people find *me* frightening.

I got in touch with Jim Griffin, an elfin figure who heads the William Morris television department in New York, and together we began a saga that lasted years to finally find a talk show for the annoying Charles Grodin to host. *Sweet* and *kind* are not words that first come to mind when describing an agent, but that's Jimmy. He also seems to have a friendly relationship with most people in show business, who are probably as surprised by his personality as I was.

I remember particularly a lunch meeting Jimmy and I had with some people from ABC. There were people there representing nighttime talk, and there were people there representing daytime talk. They were all very complimentary. They had seen me over the years as a guest on various talk shows, and thought I absolutely had what it took to host a show, but as the afternoon wore on it became clear that the daytime people thought I should be on at night, and the nighttime people thought I should be on during the day; so of course I wasn't on at all. (I wonder if they planned it that way.)

Next came a long dance with the people at Westinghouse. I met their families. I watched their kids play basketball. I told them I didn't need to be across America—one station in Buffalo (which they owned) would be okay with me for a start. After many meetings and a great deal of enthusiasm, a deal was to be negotiated the next day to do a syndicated show for Westinghouse. They never called. Later they wrote a letter explaining why, but I honestly can't remember what they said.

Finally, there was King World, the biggest syndicator of them all (*Jeopardy; Wheel of Fortune; Oprah*). Michael King was a fan and was ready to move toward a syndicated show with me.

My idea for the show was not dissimilar to *Politically Incorrect*. This was a couple of years before that show debuted. Bill Maher, the host of *Politically Incorrect,* and I are worlds apart in the sensibility department, but the idea of sitting with four or five people, preferably, in my concept, to avoid the familiar, not journalists but bright entertainers, seemed like it could be entertaining and have real value.

I now had to find someone who would run the whole show. After meeting with several people I ended up picking a producer who was extremely experienced and came well recommended. Unfortunately there was something else about him that quickly revealed itself. If anyone in any way didn't fully embrace everything he said, he would point his finger at you, as though it were a gun, and pretend to shoot you, and when he wasn't shooting someone, he looked as though he was considering blowing up the entire building.

Little by little, fewer meetings were held. The show was going forward. It's just that people tended to stay in their own offices as much as possible. I spoke to the producer once about the gun thing, and he seemed genuinely amazed that anyone would be put off by his "sense of humor." They don't call it unconscious hostility for nothing. It quickly became clear it wasn't going to work with this producer.

I've spent a lot of time trying to understand why things sometimes don't work out with people. It seems to happen everywhere to everyone. In work and in personal life it feels as though it's the norm to run into someone who acts in ways it's hard to understand.

Since in most cases I know these people to be good people, I've struggled to understand why they do what they do.

At the very beginning of my career, I was involved in a situation that to this day troubles me.

I had been an apprentice in a nonunion summer theater where I had not only worked for nothing, I actually had to pay room and board. Room was one of six cots in a garage, and board, which I guess means food, was as meager as it could be and still qualify as board. I'm talking about one small hamburger patty, a boiled potato, and about four string beans. No seconds.

However, along with all the sweeping of the theater, etc., I got to play some small parts that got bigger as the season went on.

The next year they invited me back to do a role in one of the plays. The theater had gone union in the meantime, and to work there I would be obligated to join the guild. That was a big step up, and it gave me some credibility at the beginning of my career, when you have none, just hope.

When I arrived there, the very nice grandmotherly lady in charge told me she had just learned that, because of their union status, she had to pay me seventy-five dollars a week, and the problem was that they only could afford forty.

As I write this, all these years later, amazingly I see for the first time that she probably didn't *just* learn that, but it was a plan to hit me with that when I arrived.

Rehearsal was about to begin. My choice was either to go home or give them back thirty-five dollars from the seventy-five.

In other words, they wanted a kickback. I was uneasy, but I did it. What a terrible price I paid for that. To this day it bothers me that I got into that union under false pretenses. It's true I would later have qualified, but still it's always made me feel bad about myself.

I wonder if that woman at the summer theater ever gave a moment's thought to the years of bad feeling she might cause a young person by putting me in that situation. Probably not for a second. I'm sure she was thinking only about saving her thirty-five dollars.

Of course, it was my responsibility to do the right thing, which, in hindsight, would have been to turn around, get on the bus, and go home, but I was too young and inexperienced to know that my conscience wouldn't be able to handle that I did the wrong thing.

The good news is, it was a life lesson that taught me to be more careful about my actions in the future. After all, the most important person you have to live with knows everything you do and say.

Another time I ran into someone who behaved inappropriately was when I produced the sociopolitical Simon and Garfunkel special for CBS. We hired a man to be executive producer for his expertise as well as the use of his facilities.

It soon became clear that the content of the special, which I'll later talk about, made this fellow very uncomfortable. So much so that, unknown to us, he was privately preparing his own version of the broadcast that had nothing to do with what I was doing.

His was about the making of a song, with no political or social ramifications whatsoever. If that wasn't bad enough, he completely denigrated what I was doing. At one point, he referred to it as not "airworthy." He was a real veteran in the field of documentary specials, and I was a beginner, so naturally his assessment didn't feel great.

It helped that later the broadcast was chosen to be a CBS entry in the worldwide television festival at Montreux.

Why did that producer act in such an unconscionable way? Did he know he was?

Then there were two star actors I worked with in separate movies. One was American and the other English, but each one showed up for the first day of filming and immediately began to trash the script. Obviously they had read it before agreeing to do it, and they were certainly being paid a great deal of money, but they didn't seem to see anything inappropriate in what they were doing.

When I came into television I worked with a lot of producers who were as hardworking and nice as they could be. One woman, however, who may have worked harder than anyone, unfortunately was snapping at people on a regular basis. It may have been that she was on overload, but there's no justification for that. Once, maybe, but regularly? Not for me. Soon she was snapping elsewhere in the building.

I had an odd experience with the wife of a friend of mine once at dinner. She asked me to do lines from a movie I'd been in. I chuckled, thinking I could slough it off, but she persisted. When I continued to decline, I hoped in a friendly way, she got really annoyed. "You did it in the movie!" she complained. I was never able to make the point to her that there was a difference between a movie and a dinner.

Over and over I see people behaving badly with seemingly no idea that they are. It's the parent who calls the coach to complain bitterly and profanely about his kid's playing time, seemingly unaware that in competitive sports playing time is appropriately determined by the coach's evaluation of performance.

It's human to be inappropriately self-serving, and damaging not to see it. For me, the most blatant national example of this was Bill Clinton's statement, after being forced to acknowledge his relationship with Monica Lewinsky, "Even a president is entitled to a private life." When you consider that his "private life" included oral sex with an intern in the Oval Office, there's enough lack of awareness and self-serving sentiment in that one statement to make the most avid Clinton fan shudder.

In the 2001 season the baseball manager Davey Lopes bitterly criticized opposing player Rickey Henderson for stealing a base when his team was ahead by several runs. Baseball experts pointed out that as a player, Lopes had done the same thing several times.

A neighbor of a cousin of mine peered through the window of her condo, then called her to say, "I see you're baking." What really bothered my cousin was that she already had her blinds drawn to just a little opening at the bottom for privacy. The snoop had no idea how offensive she was.

Recently there was a story in the news about one of the participants in a network reality show who held a knife to a woman's neck and "jokingly" suggested he might kill her. He, like my producer who used his finger as a gun, was startled that people didn't get his "sense of humor." He later was arrested for assaulting his girlfriend.

This odd behavior can be as basic as showing up at a friend's door without calling. I realize that's acceptable to some, but you have to know that to millions of us it's not. The examples are unending. Dear Abby and others make a good living out of dealing with this sort of thing.

If we assume that most people's intentions are not malevolent, why is there so much bad behavior in the world?

It has to be need. People's needs just blind them to reality, or allow them to easily justify what others see as offensive behavior.

I recently spoke on the phone to a friend I hadn't talked to in a long time. He was attempting to be warm and witty and charming, as he praised himself to the skies and tore me down. Later in the call I was speaking to his wife, who wanted to ask me some advice, and from the background I heard him shouting, "What do you want to ask him for?" I'd seen very little of this fellow over the years, and other friends had described him as "nakedly narcissistic." I'd always said that wasn't my experience, but now it was.

What was interesting about the conversation was the warm "package" in which all the abuse, and I don't think that's too strong a word, was coming. This man had such a need to build himself up that it became absolutely essential to diminish me to achieve his, I'm sure, unconscious goal.

The one thing most of us have in common when the problems caused by our behavior are brought to our attention is astonishment. Of course, that's understandable. If we were more aware we wouldn't have behaved badly in the first place. Sometimes it feels like "Hello, have a nice day, goodbye" is the safest way to get through life.

In trying to understand this, I realized that if this is a common human flaw, then it must be true of me as well.

I thought back to something that happened about ten years ago. At that time, and probably twenty years prior to that, I was a storyteller who seemed never to run out of stories. At every social occasion, whenever it seemed appropriate, I would launch into a story, and people enjoyed it. Eventually it kind of always seemed "appropriate." One day a very close friend of mine, as gently as he could, told me that while the stories were entertaining, others who were more laid back in a group seldom got a chance to talk. In other words, even though they were funny, my friend said there were too many stories. Another friend on hearing this was angry and said, "There's no such thing as too many funny stories!"

I fought the instinct to rebut the friend who criticized me. It took courage for him to speak to me about this. It's really ironic, because along with being a close friend, he's also about my biggest supporter. He prominently displays in his apartment, of all things, a montage of me telling a story!

Even though I was embarrassed, I listened to what my friend said and cut back on the stories. I actually cut back so much, people would look at me and wonder why I was uncharacteristically quiet. The truth is I didn't have as good a time either, but it was obviously the right thing to do.

This, I think, is a good example of my "need" to entertain often getting in the way of more appropriate behavior, and prior to my friend's speaking to me I had no inkling I had done anything inappropriate. That, I believe, is the answer to why there is so much bad behavior everywhere. We can all be unaware of a bigger picture, because we are taken over by our needs. In my case I was fortunate, because it wasn't long after my friend leveled with me that I got my own talk show, where there was plenty of room for stories. Over the years since telling stories became part of my profession, the need to do it socially really diminished. Years later, the friend who had criticized me said, "Now Chuck only talks if he's paid."

Back to the syndicated talk show. From King World headquarters, there was the ongoing suggestion to add "elements." In fairness, I'm sure they were right; this was to be an afternoon syndicated show, and four or five people sitting around talking about current events is not exactly *Judge Judy*! *Politically Incorrect*, of course, is successful in a very late-night environment where not as large an audience is required to stay on the air as in the afternoon.

After a short while, even though it wasn't what I had in mind, I decided to try to rise to the challenge of "elements." I remember coming up with the idea of sending a remote crew to cover a "story" about a horse who could type. We would go to a riding stable, put a typewriter by a horse's feet, and, of course, nothing much would happen. I was sure it was good for some laughs.

I was lying awake thinking about all this one night in a hotel room in Los Angeles, where I was on a book tour—the horse who could type—and my producer who looked like he'd like to blow up the building and I began to have some serious second thoughts.

I had appeared on *Tom Snyder* that night. Tom then had a live hour show on CNBC at ten o'clock following Geraldo Rivera. I always had a lot of fun appearing with Tom. He's never competitive and truly enjoys his guests. The next day, my representative, Jimmy Griffin, got a call asking if I'd be interested in replacing Tom on CNBC, as he was leaving to do an hour show on CBS following David Letterman. The call came from a man named Andy Friendly, who is the son of Fred Friendly, who was Edward R. Murrow's producer at CBS. Fred Friendly was a man exalted in television for his passion for taking on important social or political issues, whether they were ratings-getters or not. At one point, he worked under CBS head Jim Aubrey, who said to him that they were natural enemies, because Fred was dedicated to serving the public, and Jim was dedicated to making as much money as possible for the network. Andy Friendly had his dad's values, and this was something that would bode well for me—for a time. Of course, at the moment of the call, I was only thinking that here was a chance to go right on the air. In the best of circumstances, the King World syndicated show would be a year away. There'd be no talk of "elements" on CNBC, only talk, and as far as I knew, no producer who looked like he'd like to blow up the building.

I met with Andy Friendly. Andy, then and always, seemed to have a perpetual smile on his face. He was unendingly good-willed and exuded a benign quality that went really nicely with his kindly bear look. Andy said he saw me as "dessert" from ten o'clock to eleven, following the hard-hitting Geraldo from nine o'clock to ten. He also assured me he was dedicated to being supportive of talent. What I particularly liked about the whole thing was what Tom did at the beginning of his show. He'd look right into the camera and talk about whatever was on his mind—no TelePrompTer, just Tom on anything. That was the fascinating opportunity.

Still I was conflicted about the two choices, and as strange as it may seem, I spoke about it with my then seven-year-old son as I drove him to school. I said, "On one hand, with a syndicated show, there will be endless opportunities to do comedy, and people seem to like it when I do that. With the CNBC show, even though it was referred to as dessert, it's a business and hard-news network, hardly a place to focus that much on comedy." He thought a moment, then said from the backseat, "I don't think they'd have any problem on CNBC with you doing as much comedy as you want. I think you should go there." I immediately realized he was right, and before we got to school, I made the decision to go to CNBC.

People find it astonishing that such an exchange would take place between my seven-year-old and me, but it did. People with kids know that sometimes, even at seven, kids have more wisdom than we grown-ups.

When my son was thirteen I followed his general advice about the stock market. I'm not kidding. I won't say what it was, because who knows, at sixteen he may be putting out a booklet and getting paid for his counsel. When he was fourteen he was having his reviews of rap albums published on an international website. Please forgive this proud father for mentioning that.

We made King World aware of what was going on, and they generously agreed to let me accept CNBC's offer, retaining syndication rights and probably getting some cash from CNBC. King World's reasoning was they would have a free look at me on television. CNBC would, in effect, be a pilot for King World, if and when. The one remaining step was to meet with the number-one man at CNBC, Roger Ailes. I hadn't met Roger when he first okayed me to take over that week for Tom on *The Tomorrow Show*, so this was to be a first.

Andy Friendly took me into Roger's office. In retrospect, I benefited by not really knowing much about Roger Ailes at the time. The same was true at a later date when I met with Jack Welch.

Among other things, Roger is known as a rough-and-tumble street fighter in the media world. He's certainly not someone to cross, as he is dedicated to having the last word, which he usually gets, because he seems to be quicker and wittier than his rivals.

Over the years Roger and I have become friends. While we like each other, and share a penchant for looking for a good laugh, there is another reason we're friends. We wear each other like a badge of honor. How conservative can he be if he's friends with Charles Grodin? How liberal can I be if I'm friends with Roger Ailes?

I can't remember what was said at that first meeting except we laughed for the next two hours, and I was set to begin my career as a talk show host on CNBC. This was the end of 1994, and I was to begin in January 1995.

Steve Friedman

After Roger Ailes reads what I had to say about some of his Fox hosts, it's going to be tougher for me to get a laugh out of him.

Marty Short,
Johnny Carson, and Reviews

The next plan of action was for me to come in and do a rehearsal to see how everything worked. They had arranged for me to do an interview on the satellite with a fellow who was running their Los Angeles office. Since I was using this only to get acclimated to the technical side, I didn't intend to do a serious interview but, surprise, surprise, chose to fool around, so I asked him questions like "What's your favorite color?" and "If you were an animal, what kind of an animal would you be?" It never occurred to me that Andy Friendly and Roger Ailes were watching all this on monitors in their offices, and getting nervous. I don't think that they believed once I went on the air I'd ask people their favorite colors, but still...

After the rehearsal, I got word Andy wanted me to drop by his office. He is a very gentle man; not wanting to criticize me directly, he pointed out that while it may have appeared that Tom Snyder was winging it, he actually was walking the beach during the day thinking about the show. I nodded politely and chose not to say that in my whole professional life it's been hard to get me to *stop* working on something, not start. Ask my wife.

Before the show premiered live at ten o'clock, Andy thought it would be a good idea to tape a show to have in reserve, in case we were hit by a snowstorm and I was unable to get to the studio. I lived about an hour away.

My plan was to do each show with one guest and a singer singing the standards I loved at the end. Astonishingly, no one had ever mentioned ratings to me. The naive idea of one guest and a singer at the end now makes me smile, or should I say wince, unless of course the guest and singer were "Returning from the other side— Amelia Earhart and Elvis," although Larry King seems able to do this. Of course, I was beginning, and Larry is an institution.

My guest for the taped show in reserve was the witty storyteller Tony Randall, and the singer was Julius La Rosa, a big hit in the days of Arthur Godfrey, who fired him for lacking humility. This was ironic because "humble" would certainly not be the first word to describe Mr. Godfrey, who was a favorite of mine.

It was from Arthur Godfrey that I first heard the idea that when you're speaking to the audience on radio or television or anywhere for that matter, you should speak as though you're speaking to one person, because only one person at a time hears you. He was the best at it. I can still hear him say, "Hello. Golly it's good to be here."

It sounds like such an obvious idea, but still plenty of people in the media insist on using "a voice" to maintain a more formal manner.

I once had a meeting with an attorney. It was just he and I in a small office. He spoke in such a formal tone, I kept having to peek over my shoulder to see if a crowd had somehow formed behind me.

I tried to bring something fresh to that first taped show. Acting as though the show were live, I announced at the end of the monologue, "I now see something I should have guessed. You have to use the bathroom before you sit down to host an hour show." I then raced down the hall to the men's room, a man with a hand-held camera following, of course. I disappeared into the men's room, emerged in about thirty seconds, and raced back to the set in time to go to the commercial break. It was fun and nobody said, "Hold it! What's he doing?" In fact, no one ever did. It looked like my seven-year-old was right—no one was going to complain about too much comedy, even on a business and hard-news network.

Of course at eleven o'clock following me there was another exception to the business and hard-news concept, a show called *Real Personal,* hosted by an amiable former White House correspondent named Bob Berkowitz, who looked like a Jewish version of Clark Kent. Bob didn't turn into Superman, but he would surprise you in a different way. On his show people would discuss sex in such graphic terms you weren't always sure you had heard what you'd just heard. Bob's panelists really lent the CNBC building a different flavor.

For my first live show, I called on two friends to be the guests—Marty Short and my longtime close friend Art Garfunkel. I had met Marty on one of the last movies I had done, *Clifford,* where he played a comedically precocious ten-year-old, and I played his uncle. I had one of the best times of my life working with Marty, but what really impressed me about him was the way he chose to step into one of those sticky political situations that most people avoid. There was an ongoing power play between the production manager on that movie and some of the actors, the director, the makeup people—just about everyone. Here was a man who really tried to throw his weight around. To me, one of the most important jobs for anyone working behind the camera is to do what they can to support the people in front of the camera, and I say that as someone who's worked on both sides many times.

My problem with this production manager had to do with the morning calls to work. Since the days are regularly twelve to fourteen hours long, I'm really not crazy about being asked to show up at six A.M. and not having anyone ready to work, as I stand alone in the dark. He and I had a real tug of war over this, and we had an uneasy relationship. It wasn't as bad as his relationships with some of the other people, who outright despised him, but it was not good. Eventually others had him barred from the set for the peace of mind of the company, but he tried to take revenge on me by arranging the schedule so that I wouldn't be finished in time to fly home for Thanksgiving. Marty Short's manager was the producer of the movie, so Marty had some extra clout. Marty called a meeting and told everyone I regularly rewrote scenes—in his opinion to excellent advantage. (The original writers were not involved with the movie because of problems that took place before I was there.) Marty said I helped in a number of extracurricular ways, never asked for any money, and he felt they should try to accommodate me—and they did. That might not sound that unusual, but I seldom see anyone step up to anything when they can avoid it. I've always had a high regard for Marty for doing that.

I met Art Garfunkel in the movie *Catch-22* and later became close friends with both him and Paul Simon, and Art agreed to be the first show's singer. In 1969, when I made the Simon and Garfunkel special for CBS, it dealt with many of the social issues I later dealt with in my show, but at this point I was primarily thinking about comedy and music—"dessert."

In five years, there were only a couple of occasions when I would speak to a guest before the show, and this first program was one of them. I called Marty and asked him to do the whole appearance as Katharine Hepburn and to take the position that she had no idea who I was and, when she did, that she didn't care for me. Marty asked, "You mean you don't mind if I attack you any way I want?" "Absolutely," I said. I could almost hear him grinning on the other end of the phone.

Here are some of the exchanges from that first show with Marty on the satellite from L.A. (Throughout the introduction, we see Marty as Hepburn holding his earpiece in a quizzical manner.)

Me: With me now is a woman who is one of the nation's most beloved screen actresses. She is the first woman to ever win four Academy Awards. Her career on stage and screen has stretched over five decades. Her film credits include many of the great movies: *The Philadelphia Story, Woman of the Year, Adam's Rib, Pat and Mike, Guess Who's Coming to Dinner, The Lion in Winter,* and *On Golden Pond.* It's with the deepest pleasure that I welcome screen legend Katharine Hepburn. Welcome, Miss Hepburn, to my first show. Can you hear...

Marty as Hepburn (holding up earpiece): I don't...I don't...I don't...I don't know what this is.... What do I do with this?

Me: Somebody help...

Marty as Hepburn: One, two, three, I can't hear a thing. I can't hear a bloody thing.

Me: Can you put...Miss Hepburn, if you put it in your ear. Can you put the ear plug in your ear? Can you hear me?

Marty as Hepburn: Who are you?

Me: Hi. Welcome and thank you...

Marty as Hepburn: Hello. Who are you? I don't know who I'm talking to. I don't have a clue!

Me: It's Charles Grodin. It's the premiere show. Did you see *Midnight Run?* I was...

Marty as Hepburn: Midnight Run with De Niro and a very bland person who played opposite. I don't like De Niro.

Me: That was me.

Marty as Hepburn: He cusses, and I don't get it. Why must he swear, and there's a lot of bravado. I don't understand it. Spencer would swear, but he had the decency to wait until someone said, "Wrap," and he'd say, "What the hell, this isn't tea with lemon," and he'd throw it down. Sometimes I'd say, "Oh, Spencer, for God's sake you don't understand that you're being..." They don't understand that inside this anger there's a teddy bear. (*To me*) Is that who you are? Who are you?

Me: No, have you ever, I've been on the David Letterman show, the Johnny Carson show. Have you ever seen me on those?

Marty as Hepburn: Oh God, you're not that dreadful person who is so angry. I don't like you, I find you dull. I think you're a pleasant face in a roundish sort of way, but I find your personality very unappealing.

Me: That's just a comic bit that I was doing with Letterman and Carson—just a comic bit.

Marty as Hepburn: Oh, then I'm intrigued. I can't wait to come back.

After about a week of doing the show, I was reviewed by just about every major publication, and the reviews were outstanding, the ones I was aware of anyway.

There was one review that really got my attention.

I began the show by getting off a bus outside the building muttering to myself, "Welcome to the broadcast. Welcome to the telecast. Welcome to the show." It was an idea I had because Andy Friendly kept reminding me not to say it was a broadcast or a program or something that didn't have to do with cable, and I could never remember what it was or wasn't. I then entered the lobby of the building to be intercepted by Phil Donahue, who gave me the idea for this opening. Phil, by the way, is about the most giving person I've ever met in my life. It's remarkable to me how many funerals, weddings, and birthdays he will show up for, no matter where they are, not to mention countless charitable events. He had a show on CNBC for a time with Vladimir Posner, the Russian commentator. With deliberately loud marching music drowning out the dialogue, Phil appeared to be giving me a pep talk, as he walked me to the elevator. Once on the elevator, Bob Berkowitz, who hosted the show on sex, spotted me and whispered intently into my ear, and when I emerged there was Geraldo Rivera giving me various versions of high fives. I then hurried down the hall and onto the set, where Andy Friendly took my coat, and said I was late. I hurried into my seat, explained to the audience the bus was stuck in traffic on the George Washington Bridge, and apologized. Of course, everything but the walk down the hall into the studio had been pretaped, and in reality I'd been at the studio for about ten hours. One reviewer commented that he really liked the show, but did remonstrate with me a little for arriving late!

I got a call from Roger Ailes after the show, and he said he felt that it was one of the funniest television shows he'd ever seen. On the other hand, I was out in Los Angeles shortly after that having dinner with Johnny Carson and his wife, Alex, and he said, "Too much Hepburn." Alex quickly responded, "Oh, c'mon, John, you were laughing!"

In my twenty years appearing with Johnny, I had never seen him out of the studio until that dinner. I once said to him on the air that what was really stressful for me wasn't appearing, it was what do you say if you run into him in the makeup room where everyone hoped to be witty. I told him I had prepared lines for offstage, not on. It was a joke, but it was not a walk in the park running into him, even though he was always incredibly friendly. David Letterman, for example, I've never seen offstage, but I've gotten warm notes from him. Jay Leno, on the other hand, comes into your dressing room and shmoozes with you before the show, then goes out and personally warms up the audience. He tours on weekends. He also couldn't be nicer. (I'm starting to sound like the clichéd talk show guest I tried to avoid being.)

When Johnny invited me to dinner, I was flattered and looked forward to sharing with him all that was going on with the hosting. As I told him about everything, he didn't even pretend to be interested. He was really nice and funny, just not that interested. This was not that long after he'd retired from a lifetime in television, and I've had a similar reaction to people talking to me about movies, after I got out. At one point, I looked at him and for fun said, "What do *you* find interesting?" He then proceeded to tell me about some rare event that was coming up in the field of astronomy. I looked at him and said, "You can't seriously find that more interesting than show-biz anecdotes!"

At one point he talked about safaris he and Alex liked to go on, and seemed to be suggesting I come along. I said something like,

"You mean sleep in a tent in the middle of the jungle and have dangerous animals maybe try to get in and kill you?"

That would have been something though, lying in a tent in the middle of the jungle with a guy I used to be wary of running into backstage at NBC!

Based on that dinner, it was clear Johnny didn't want to talk about television, but there were some people he'd known only as guests on television that he wouldn't mind seeing again, hence dinner. (I always wanted to use the word *hence* in a sentence.)

A few years ago, I received some residuals for use of my appearances on *The Tonight Show* in cassette collections. There were three checks that totaled about eight dollars. Seriously! I wrote to Johnny and said, "I always thought I was a tiny part of the success of *The Tonight Show*, I just hadn't realized how tiny." He wrote back, and said he'd looked into it, and in fact, it turned out to have been an overpayment that would be deducted from any future check.

Happy Times

This was a wonderful time for me at CNBC. No one even mentioned ratings and, of course, I never thought about them. It wouldn't be too long before I'd be forced to confront the issue, but all I thought about then was getting the best guests to do the best shows.

Carol Burnett was one of my first guests. Carol and I had become good friends years earlier when I made my second effort to contribute something on a national level. The first was in the late 1960s, when I made the Simon and Garfunkel special for CBS. Simon and Garfunkel were at their peak then, and I persuaded them to use the program to put the spotlight on the unprotected people in America. That prompted a line from the man representing the ad agency for the sponsor, AT&T, that I'll never forget. He said to me, "You're using our money to sell your ideology!" I asked him, "What's my ideology?" and he responded, "The humanistic approach!" After a moment when I realized he wasn't kidding, I said naively (I was in my thirties), "You mean there are people who are against the humanistic approach?" He quickly said, "You're goddamned right there are!" AT&T eventually removed its name from the special, I guess anticipating it would offend people in the South because of its pro-integration stance.

A little later I happened to be seated with some friends near this fellow at a restaurant, and we overheard him talking about me. He said, "Simon and Garfunkel are under the spell of this Svengali guy, Charles Grodin." A friend of mine piped up to let him know I was sitting right there, and both groups continued their dinner with an unusual amount of silence and no further Svengali talk. The truth was, it didn't take much persuasion for me to get Paul and Art to do the show, since their values mirrored mine anyway.

I went on to the movies after that, and it was about ten years later when I felt compelled to speak up about whatever I could to try to make the country a better place. If I sound like a Pollyanna, you'd be surprised how many of us there are like that.

In any case, Carol Burnett and I went out for dinner one night and I began to talk to her about an idea I had. It struck me that there were relatively few people I knew who put a premium on how friendly we are to one another. Since Carol was one of them, I knew I'd have a receptive ear. Too many people seemed to be solely about making money or making a name for themselves. Possibly because of this, we seemed to be becoming a meaner society. When I first began to talk about this, more than one of my friends thought I was joking, and when they realized I wasn't, they let me know how boring they thought it was. This sentiment, without fail, came from friends who could most benefit from looking at their own behavior but, of course, didn't.

Carol embraced the concept with even more enthusiasm than I, and I immediately called Phil Donahue. When I proposed his doing an hour on friendliness, there was a silence on the other end of the phone. I quickly said, "Phil, the audience will be interested in anything Carol Burnett has to say." Without missing a beat, he booked us into a large amphitheater in upstate New York. After the broadcast, we received more than ten thousand pieces of mail! My mother and her girlhood friend Ann Baker opened every one of them and sent our reply. They had a small two-bedroom apartment in the Valley in Los Angeles, and every surface was covered with mail and tapes and prayers that were sent. We were then booked on *The Merv Griffin Show* for the full ninety minutes, and I'm still not sure whether he was kidding, but Merv seemed to be against all this friendliness! Indignantly, he said, "If a waiter spills hot soup on me, I'm supposed to be friendly?!" Carol said, "Yes, because the waiter probably feels terrible already."

There was an article in *The Village Voice* by a caustic critic named James Wolcott, who seemed furious that I particularly was going around telling people to be friendly. He said I looked like the kind of person who could steal food off your plate when you weren't looking. The *Voice* gave me a page to respond, and I admitted that about twenty years ago I had, in fact, taken a slice of tomato off a friend's plate, but I had changed over the years, and I'd never done anything like that again.

After those appearances, we gave interviews on the subject, and thousands wanted to join our organization, but we didn't have an organization—it was just a consciousness raiser. I do know that certain groups were formed around the country espousing friendliness, but after a while Carol and I went back to working for a living. Looking back, I can't say that the country got any friendlier because of our efforts. Clearly it seems to have gotten meaner, now dominated by so much hate radio, and yet who knows? I really appreciate what the writer Henry James said when asked the three most important things in life: "Be kind. Be kind. Be kind."

When the time came to put together a first week of guests, I reached out to Carol. I knew she'd respond positively in spite of what had happened the last time I'd seen her.

I was out in Los Angeles and called her to have dinner. I went to her house to pick her up. It was on a night that Mike Tyson was defending his heavyweight championship in Japan against an unknown fighter named Buster Douglas, who was as big an underdog as you can be and still get the fight. It came on television, and I said to Carol, who was all set to head to the restaurant, "Hold on a second, this fight will be over real quick." It went on and on as Carol in her nice Carol way kind of stared at me. Finally, Buster knocked Mike out in one of the biggest upsets in the history of boxing. We were significantly delayed getting to the restaurant. Through it all, you couldn't even call Carol "perturbed." That's just one of the reasons she's been America's sweetheart through most of her adult life.

The next day she called me to say that all anyone was talking about at the studio was the fight, implying that she was really grateful to me that we'd watched it.

The fun times continued on the show with the appearance of two star comic actors. In the mid-1980s, I did a very funny low-budget movie called *Last Resort* with two unknown comedy actors, Jon Lovitz and Phil Hartman. They were about to audition for *Saturday Night Live,* so I phoned my friend Lorne Michaels to give him a heads-up on these two guys, whom others had called about as well. They were extraordinarily gifted, and happily Lorne saw it.

Carol Burnett and I with Phil Donahue, promoting friendliness. We got ten thousand pieces of positive mail in response to this broadcast, even though some of my less friendly friends thought it was a boring subject or that I was joking.

They would always do my show whenever I asked, and they were always hilarious.

When Phil's life was taken, for me it was surreal, as I know it was for all his friends. Some things never get real, no matter how much time passes, and this is one of them for me.

Of course, Phil was a brilliant actor, but what I also always remember about him was how kind he was to everyone.

With Jon Lovitz just as with Marty Short, I made another rare exception to my rule of never speaking to a guest before an appearance. We would throw around some ideas for a bit we could do. As far as I can remember, those two fellas were the only ones I spoke with beforehand. Some of the serious guests asked to speak with me before an appearance, but I always thought it better to have all conversation on the air. There was some going back and forth among my staff and Barry Scheck, one of O. J. Simpson's lawyers, about his appearing with me. I had been highly critical of his actions in the Simpson trial. Here was a man using DNA evidence to free innocent people with his Innocence Project, and now it seemed to me he was using his expertise to free a guilty man, and he knew it. He claims the Simpson case problem was about handling the DNA, not the DNA itself, but to the layman that's a murky distinction, particularly since it's hard to believe he didn't know he was working to free a double murderer. That someone who has dedicated his life to freeing innocent people would work for O. J. Simpson is mind-boggling. He said he was interested in appearing with me, if I would speak to him on the phone privately first. I refused, and he never appeared.

Since Jon Lovitz, as far as I know, never had any association with O. J. Simpson, I did speak with him, and we worked out some outlines of what we'd do. The appearance about to be recounted followed an earlier appearance in which I commented on how much weight Jon had gained. He defended himself by allowing how he had gained fifty pounds over a five-year period while working on *Saturday Night Live* and eating late at night, but he was in the process of taking it off, because his intention was to play romantic leads. I expressed astonishment at his intention, and said he'd more likely be successful if he would continue to head in the other direction, where we really only had Dom DeLuise (who when I asked him on the air if there was anything he *wouldn't* eat, without missing a beat, said, "Hooves").

Anyway, in a previous appearance, Jon on the satellite (as planned) took great umbrage at the Dom DeLuise reference (and earlier references to Jon as a "fat pig"), stood up, threw a doughnut he had been munching on at the camera, and stormed off the set. The following recounts his next appearance with me.

Me (to camera): In his last appearance, Jon Lovitz was clearly upset. I phoned him, and he didn't return my call, and I phoned him some more; and finally we talked and he agreed to come back on and now, oddly enough, Jon's back and he's got a diet book and an exercise video! It's fine with me. His friendship is more important to me than anything, so if we could go to the satellite we have Jon Lovitz live in Los Angeles.

(We see Jon on the monitor smiling, waving, and flashing a V for victory sign with his fingers. He is dressed in black.)

Me: Hi, good to see you. Great to see you. Glad that we're back together. I understand you have a new diet book and an exercise video. What is the diet?

Jon: You're saying to me "You need to lose weight" and everything, and I watched the tape, and I said, "Ya know, he's right," and I really got into it, and I lost about twenty pounds.

Me: You've lost twenty pounds since the last appearance?! You must have lost it in an area we're not seeing now.

(Jon stares at the camera.)

Me: I mean that in a totally friendly way!

Jon (sarcastically): Everybody's a comedian!

Me (apologetically): No ... no ... no.

Jon: Anyway ...

Me: Yeah ...

Jon: So I have this book out. Remember the video *Buns of Steel*?

Me: The exercise video. Right.

Jon: It's like that, but not really. The diet book and the video are just called *Buns.*

Me: Buns.

Jon: Buns. You know, eat the buns and work on your buns.

Me: So you're tying in the name of the diet with the actual buttocks, in effect.

Jon: Yes. Everyone says diets don't work, but they do if you stick with them.

Me: Yes.

Jon: Diet means what? *(superarticulation)* It means how you eat.

Me: Yes, how you eat.

Jon: So what you do ... *(superarticulation)* For breakfast you can have a slice of melon, a slice of honeydew, and eight ounces of orange juice, and that's it.

Me: A little bit of melon, a little bit of juice for breakfast. That's good.

Jon: That gets everything going, the metabolism starting up and everything.

Me: Yeah.

Jon: Then for lunch...(*superarticulation*) one half cup of cottage cheese.

Me: Right.

Jon (*superarticulation*)*:* And three pieces of melba toast.

Me: Melba toast.

Jon: But it has to be melba toast, it can't be wheat or rye, because three pieces of melba toast is like a whole piece of bread.

Me: You're kind of like a diet authority. All this in the last three weeks. Did you do a big study of this?

Jon: Yeah, I met with doctors, nutritionists.

Me: I see. So not only do you have the book, but you have the tape. So it's the melon, the juice in the morning and the toast, the melba toast, of course. Anything on the melba toast?

Jon: No.

Me: Just the melba toast?

Jon: That's it. You want to lose weight, don't you?

Me: I don't. I'm fine. (*Jon seems to take offense.*) No. No, of course... It's more important we stay friends. What about dinner?

Jon: Well now...here's the beauty of it. For dinner you can eat absolutely anything you want with one diet item, but you can only eat for one minute—so here you can see...

(*Camera pulls back to reveal food on a table in front of Jon.*)

It's dinnertime here—I have boysenberry pie....

(*We see one piece missing from the pie.*)

I ate some last night—that's leftover. Then I have fries, a cheeseburger, and the diet item is a Diet Coke.

Me: Yes. So you can eat as much as you want of that in one minute? Well, it's dinnertime in Los Angeles.

(Jon puts his hand on his forehead.)

What, are you getting yourself in the mood?

Jon: No, I'm just faint from not eating all day.

Me: Okay. Do you have a watch? Do you want us to time this?

Jon: Yeah. You time it. Give me a minute and say, "Go," and I'll just show you. It's quite enjoyable.

Me: Okay, go!

Jon (delicately picking up one french fry): I'm enjoying my meal and I'm chewing properly. Mmmm. *(He accelerates his pace, taking a bite out of the cheeseburger and another fry.)*

(A little frantic) How much time?

Me: Thirty seconds.

Jon (digging into the pie) (with mouth full) (more frantic): How much time? How much time!

Me: You've got twenty seconds.

(Jon picking up whole pie pan and taking a big bite.)

(I look repulsed.)

Jon: How much time? How much time!

Me: You've got fifteen seconds!

Jon (desperately eating burger, fries, and pie): How much time?

Me: You've got five seconds. You want a drink, so you won't choke to death?

Jon (shouting): How much time!

Me: You've got ... You're finished! You're finished!

Jon (coughing, sputtering, almost choking—points to food): Take it away! Take it away!

Me: Somebody please take the food away, because he'd go for it.

(A stagehand quickly removes the food.)

    Take the Diet Coke! Oh, I guess the Diet Coke is okay.

Jon: No, take it away!

(A silence as Jon composes himself.)

Me: That's wonderful, and the title of the book and the tape...

Jon: Buns.

Me: Jon Lovitz's Buns.

Jon: Now I'd like to plug my show *The Critic.* It's coming on this Sunday night right after *The Simpsons.* It's an animated cartoon. Also, my character will be on *The Simpsons,* you see.

(I'm staring at him.)

So I'll be on *The Simpsons* as Jay Sherman, the critic, and then my own show. It's going to be very funny and then also this Monday...

(He reaches down for a bag and pulls out a large chocolate chip cookie and begins to eat it.)

    I'm going to be on the American Comedy Awards on ABC and I hope you watch....

Me: Excuse me. Excuse me! Aren't we past the one-minute deadline? *(pointing to cookie)* What's that?

Jon (nonchalant): Yes?

Me: What are you doing?

Jon (with great impatience, mouth filled with cookie): This is a reward for training! Helloooo!!?

Me (looking exasperated): Yeah, yeah. Okay. So this is your diet? You eat as much...

Jon (interrupting, annoyed): This has nothing to do with the diet! This is from the training. You get a reward. The diet's over.

Me (exploding): You're a fat pig! You've got to stop this! You come in here, you eat, you stuff your face, you plug... what is this, a cartoon?

Jon (easily): It's called *The Critic.* It's on after *The Simpsons* on Sunday. Then I'm on the American Comedy Awards—

Me (interrupting, furious): Oh, please! Kill the satellite! Kill the satellite! Kill the satellite!

(The monitor goes black.)

Jon continued to appear with me over the years, and I always felt he was as funny as anyone gets.

Snapshots and More

Morgan Fairchild came on, and I talked about the time the Playboy Channel flew in a whole crew to New York from Los Angeles to interview Morgan, who was ill and couldn't appear. Someone reached me and asked if I could do them a favor and fill in since the crew was all set up with no one to interview. I remembered a visit to the Playboy Mansion years ago with, of all people, Warren Beatty. Hugh Hefner couldn't have been nicer, so I agreed. When I got to the theater where they were set up for the interview, the producer said to me apologetically that he hadn't had time to do any research, and could I fill him in on what I'd been up to lately. I said I was a little uncomfortable telling him all about myself, and why didn't he just go ahead and ask me whatever questions he had for Morgan, and he did. Here's one exchange:

Interviewer: Do you feel you're as sexy as Loni Anderson?
Me: In my own way, yes.

I always had a lot of fun when my path crossed with Dr. Ruth. I first met her when I appeared on a cable show she was hosting on the Lifetime channel. She came into the green room and marched right over to me. She came up a little higher than my waist but peered right up and gave me a very penetrating look in the eye. She stared at me a few seconds, then said, "My producer told me you give hosts a hard time [the Carson reputation had preceded me], but you don't seem like a bad guy to me." I assured her she had nothing to worry about, but when I went on, and she started in with "climax" and "orgasm," I just stared at her in astonishment and said, *"Are we on the air?"*

When she came on my show, she was selling some sex book or tape where she cited her four necessities in sex—foreplay, arousal, orgasm, and after-play, which again leads to arousal, etc. The camera again just showed me staring at her in shock. She then looked at me and said, "Chuck, how do I know that you're the kind of man who just makes love and falls asleep with no after-play?" I heatedly denied the accusation, claiming, "After-play is my thing! The problem with me is I skip all the other stuff!" Dr. Ruth's amazing. There was a picture of her recently in *People* magazine in which she was in a kayak on a river dispensing all this orgasm info.

The comedy continued with Dana Carvey making a memorable appearance as President Clinton. "I'm a good president, but I'm a horny president. I like the line-item veto, and I like sex. I like troop deployment, and I like sex." This was long before the Monica Lewinsky mess.

I did an elaborate bit with Conan O'Brien's gifted sidekick, Andy Richter. Conan's show taped Andy and me at a cocktail lounge in New Jersey where I was trying to lure him away from Conan to join me: "More money, bigger audience, eventually take over." Then, we taped Andy on the set with me, trying out chairs, where it was revealed that his real interest was using his relationship with me as a stepping-stone into the movies. When I told him I had no plans to return to the movies, he stalked off in a huff. Conan then confronted Andy with the "secret undercover tape" on his show. It was all very funny. What really made the whole bit fascinating was the fact that a couple of years later, Andy announced he'd be leaving the Conan O'Brien show to pursue a career in the movies.

Frank Sinatra, Jr., appeared and did some funny fat jokes. His band had nicknames for their fat members that were takeoffs on world leaders' names, like "Yessir U Are Fat." He got one of the highest ratings we ever received. Even though he was very entertaining, the consensus was that a certain portion of the audience thought they were tuning in to see his dad.

It's, of course, helpful if you're going to be a talk show host if you're the kind of person who is interested in what people have to say. Amazingly, there are many hosts who aren't particularly interested, but can get through an hour without revealing it. I am fortunate in that I am interested. I have very little ability to participate in chitchat in life, but if I set the agenda of what is discussed, I can't recall ever not being interested in hearing what guests have to say. Also, I found if you're polite and genuine in your interest, you can ask about almost anything without offending. I remember asking the late John Denver why he chose to chainsaw some of the furniture in the home he had formerly shared with his wife. Without seeming even remotely taken aback, he calmly explained that she had cut down a number of beautiful trees he loved that were part of a cherished view. It's amazing where love can go.

When I was informed that the actress Crystal Bernard had had a date once with Rush Limbaugh, I'm afraid I fell back on an old flaw of mine, unrelentingly revisiting an unwanted subject for humor. I made reference to Crystal dating Rush so many times, Crystal looked like she wanted to jump through the monitor and throttle me. I admire that she kept her good humor, even though clearly it wasn't entirely what she was feeling.

Jerry Seinfeld made a rare cable appearance with me, and I asked him if really wealthy people had to work out. He said, "Nah, the genes know there's money there."

Cal Thomas, the conservative commentator, came on, and I was certain we would get into a political debate. Instead, he asked if he could sing, and gave a decent rendition of "Sunrise, Sunset" from *Fiddler on the Roof.*

I had Charlton Heston on the show. This was before he stood in front of the NRA and, referring to someone maybe trying to take away his gun, shouted, "From my cold dead hand." *Cold dead hand,* there's a fun phrase for you.

Some people who are against any kind of gun legislation are convinced safety locks and background checks are just the beginning of outlawing guns. Personally, like most people, I'd like to see as few guns as possible, and every protection so kids and criminals can't get their hands on them, but I would absolutely be for people owning guns for legitimate reasons.

Anyway, I didn't get into any of that with Mr. Heston. I mostly remember us talking about an affectionate nickname his grandson calls him. Clearly all of us have a lot of sides.

With the singer Lou Rawls, I chose not to mention the time I saw him in an airport and said, "You sing like you talk." I can see now that's a fairly obscure observation, but I meant it as a compliment that he has a unique style of talking and singing. However I meant it, Lou looked at me like I'd just taken a dig at him.

It reminds me of the time around thirty years ago when, late at night, on the Upper West Side of New York, I passed Sidney Poitier on the sidewalk. As I walked by him I said, "You do nice work." He wheeled around and said challengingly, "What did you say?" I repeated what I'd said, he smiled, thanked me, and walked on.

Angie Dickinson bristled in a friendly way when I asked her about Frank Sinatra, whom she used to date. She smiled, but didn't answer. I said, "I'm just asking how he acts in a restaurant. Was he nice to waiters?" Angie continued to smile and stare at me.

No one gave me an off-limits on Sinatra, and I'd read Angie's comments on Frank earlier, so I figured it was okay, but evidently not. I would never ask anyone a question about romance, but restaurant manners, absolutely!

Just before Yasmine Bleeth, who rose to fame and fortune on *Baywatch*, sat down to be interviewed, one of my staff told me, "She doesn't want to talk about *Baywatch*." I thought it was a weird request, but I skipped referring to the one thing she was known for.

I teased the entertainer Bobby Short about his pronunciation of the word *France*. Bobby gave it a broad *a*. I'm sure he's right. After all, he's spent a lot of time there, but I teased him anyway. He chuckled good-naturedly the first couple of times I did it, but by the third time he did an Angie Dickinson on me.

I asked the critic Rex Reed why he was so mean-spirited in his reviews. He smiled, not believing I was serious. When he realized I wasn't kidding he denied he was mean-spirited, but he was.

The wonderful comedy actor Leslie Nielsen came on the program. I knew he liked to squeeze something in his pocket that made the sound of flatulence. He particularly enjoyed doing it in elevators. I was hoping he wouldn't do it on the show, but he did. I chose to act as though nothing had happened, hoping he wouldn't go for it again, and he didn't. Of course, he could just as easily have kept doing it until he got the desired reaction. In that case, we at least would have had a column item.

Kathie Lee Gifford spoke openly about her differences with her producer, Michael Gelman. We released clips to all the entertainment-news shows. The newspapers also picked it up, and Kathie Lee vowed never to return to the show. She didn't, either, but she and I remained friendly, mostly because I defended her in a subsequent blowup with someone else.

Peter Ustinov spoke of appearing on a German talk show where they were fine with him not saying ahead of time what he would talk about. He quoted them as saying, "We're excited that you will improvise, but would you mind telling us exactly *what* you will improvise?"

The former Dodgers manager Tommy Lasorda and I had a good time. A few years later when I ran into him at the New York Mets training camp and introduced him to my wife, he said to her, "My condolences."

The animal trainer Jim Fowler came on, and as a gag I had one of my producers, Clay Dettmer, sit between Jim and the wild animals, and me. Well, it was partially a gag.

Buddy Hackett told about making personal appearances and warning the groups ahead of time that he worked blue. They said no problem, they loved him. When he showed up and did his thing, more than a few of the folks raced to the exits.

On the other hand, David Brenner felt he in some part owed the longevity of his career to the fact that he never worked blue.

New York's Mayor Giuliani came on around the time some New York policemen were charged with unruly behavior at some vacation spot. I think some of them were sliding down banisters naked. Hey, it's a job with a lot of pressure! Naturally, I asked the mayor all about it. During a commercial break, his press representative came over and asked me if I would mind changing the subject, reasoning correctly that there was more to being mayor of New York than commenting on naked cops.

The most controlling guest I ever had was the Charles Manson prosecutor Vincent Bugliosi. He had researched and prepared his observations on specific issues. He very much tried to get my staff to get me to stay on those subjects, which I did, allowing, of course, for my own questions, which sometimes were off his points. Vincent didn't particularly love those, and he later made sure we felt his displeasure. With all of that, we never had a more compelling guest.

With Jerry Van Dyke I remembered the time we worked together on the miniseries *Fresno*. Jerry kept asking if I thought the show felt like it was going to be a hit. Around the third time he asked, I said, "Well, what do you think?" He said, "It doesn't matter what I think, because I've never been in a hit."

I asked the basketball star Chris Webber to sign one of his photos to my then eight-year-old son, with the inscription "I really respect your inside game." Five years later my kid played for the number-one-seeded team of thirteen-year-olds in Connecticut; they went to the national finals. He has a nice inside game, too.

Phyllis Diller was a guest. A few years later I was seated next to her at a dinner party, and for fun I whispered incredibly romantic ideas in her ear. She looked at me and said, "I'm eighty-two, and just had my hip replaced." I told her I didn't care. We had a good laugh.

The French chef Jacques Pepin amazingly let me do a bit where I tasted what he prepared and had plenty of complaints. "Oh, this is *way* too salty!"

Larry King seemed genuinely taken aback that I had so many problems with O. J. Simpson's "dream team."

Gene Hein, the father of Brandon Hein, appeared. Brandon is serving a life sentence without possibility of parole for being involved in a drunken fight where one teenager stabbed another to death. Even though another boy did the stabbing, Brandon is serving a harsher sentence than Charles Manson. This is because of California's felony-murder rule. The conviction was for murder committed in the course of a robbery. My outrage over this is because not only did Brandon not kill anyone, there also was no robbery. Many of us believe this shameful sentence came about because the victim was a policeman's son, and because the trial took place shortly after the O. J. Simpson acquittal. Sometimes our justice system is shocking.

Marty Short made a later appearance. This time I didn't speak to him ahead of time but said on the satellite, "I understand, since I've seen you, you've taken up lion taming. How many times have you been bitten?" He thought a moment, then said, "Four, when it *really* hurt."

Ann Coulter, the former federal prosecutor and professional Clinton hater, came on just prior to the impeachment hearings. I asked her if she would prefer the president not be found guilty of serious charges. She looked surprised by the question, then said, "Yes, of course." Shortly after that, her book on why Clinton should be impeached was published. She later went on to distinguish herself with the following quotes. To a disabled Vietnam vet: "People like you caused us to lose that war" (MSNBC, October 11, 1997); "If you don't hate Clinton and the people who labored to keep him in office, you don't love your country" (*George*, July 1999). There's plenty more, but how much do we have to hear to know it's time to stop listening?

Alec Baldwin looked uncomfortable when I asked him about childhood fights with one of his brothers. Only later did I learn of pending assault charges against him by a photographer.

Esther Williams talked about how Tarzan, Johnny Weissmuller, used to try to grope her in underwater movie scenes. Later she wrote a book and talked about how a macho movie star she was involved with used to like to wear dresses. If you're a macho movie star who likes to wear dresses, do you worry someday it will be written about, or is that the last thing you think of when you're a man putting on a dress?

Mary Tyler Moore told the audience we had once checked into a hotel together very late at night. After a minute of looks back and forth between us, it was revealed we just happened to be on the same flight.

Farrah Fawcett mischievously wanted the audience to know she and I had been in bed together. We had, too, in a movie.

Senator John McCain was a regular guest, and I guess because I felt I knew him, I foolishly started calling him "John." Once, to be sure I wasn't being rude, I asked if he minded if I called him John. He answered, "You always call me John." I never called him John again. I told a friend of mine that story, and he said, "Well, maybe he didn't mind," but I think he did. You had to be there.

Maybe no shows provoked more strong feelings on both sides than the ones I did with the medium James Van Praagh, who claims to talk to deceased people. James has had two books on the best-seller lists for long periods and was the best-known medium in the field at that time. He worked in the mailroom of the William Morris Agency and was an aspiring screenwriter before he was trained to do what he does. A friend of mine once looked at me hard in the eye and said, "You don't seriously believe any of this, do you?" Before I could answer, he added, "You can't!" There are debunkers galore who make strong cases against Van Praagh and others who claim the same ability.

I chose not to have him use me as a subject. If I'm going to be put in communication with a deceased loved one, I would choose to do it in private rather than on national television. The emotions involved here could be overwhelming, and while "unexpected" television can be stunning, there's a limit to how much even I am interested in the unexpected.

Of course, if I had a desperate need for that kind of communication and didn't have access to a private session, I'd be out there on TV with everyone else who's looking to hear from the departed.

Most people are fascinated with all this, and my interest is probably more than most. I don't know if it's still around—it probably is—but there used to be an institute in New York for the study of the paranormal. The actor Dan Aykroyd was involved with it, and out of that eventually came the movie *Ghostbusters*.

Many years ago, I was put in touch with a woman who was connected to this organization. She did studies by, among other things, taking people who might be "endowed with special abilities" to houses that were reported to be haunted.

I went to visit her at her house in Los Angeles. I had, of course, given her my name on the phone. When I got out of my car, she looked at me and said, "It *is* you," as though that were some kind of proof of something.

In what was a test, I think, to see if I was a good candidate to go on a tour to a house reported to be inhabited by spirits, she asked me if I'd ever felt there was unseen presence in a room. Not wanting to fail the test, I said, "Sure." There were other questions of a similar nature, which I seemed to answer to her satisfaction, but for reasons I don't recall I never went to the haunted house. Being well above average in the emotionally impressionable department, I see the whole thing as a potentially life-altering experience. I am fascinated and wary at the same time. I can see a point in the future when I would subject myself to this.

I did two separate shows with Van Praagh and John Edward, and had friends on who felt they were given such specific details that it changed their lives in regard to their feelings about their lost loved ones. One young woman friend came on and Van Praagh casually said, "You have two brothers, right?" She does. He then said her mother was particularly worried about someone named Jhon (that's the way his parents spelled it). I knew my friend's mother, and even I knew she was particularly worried about her nephew Jhon (more than anyone in the world). I "lean" toward belief in Van Praagh and Edward. This comes under the heading of "what does it cost?" The vehemence, though, on both sides is profound—although certainly no more so than with abortion or capital punishment. Issues of life and death do bring out strong feelings.

Also on the serious side, I had as a guest Mary Schiavo, the former inspector general at the Department of Transportation. Mary appeared a number of times to point out that not only car companies but airlines factored how much a lawsuit would cost as against the cost to fix a potentially dangerous problem. Amazing.

We did shows on domestic violence, and I was gratified to hear that calls to the National Domestic Violence Hotline would jump way up when we gave the number, 1-800-799-SAFE. Television does have the ability to save lives, or at least change them, which again makes me shudder when I think of the 100 percent emphasis by some on ratings.

The Comedy of Discomfort

My longtime close friend Richard Martini made several appearances on the satellite as my "Hollywood correspondent." The joke was he never had any real news. He reported the split of Elizabeth Taylor and Larry Fortensky several months after the event. When I pointed out that that happened long ago, Richard looked startled, then said, "Oh really?" He spoke of going to a big opening of a Julia Roberts movie and "how lovely Julia looked," but she was whisked away by her handlers before Richard could speak to her. Some people found this hilarious, while others, like my mother and the cameraman in Los Angeles, thought it was just not ready for cable. This was, of course, the comedy of discomfort that I often practiced as a guest.

One of the reasons why the comedy of discomfort always appealed to me is that, unlike other kinds of comedy, you could absolutely count on it.

You wouldn't necessarily be sure people would find it funny, of course, but it was never dull.

The most intense comedy of discomfort we did on the show was in a series of producers' snits.

Whenever it seemed appropriate, I tried to take situations that were going on around the show and turn them into comedy segments where I would "confront" a producer on the air, and he or she would walk off in a "snit."

After the Angie Dickinson interview where Angie seemed uncomfortable when I asked about Frank Sinatra, I spoke to my producer Alice Hurwit off the air, who, of course, was as surprised as I was that the subject was off-limits. This turned into an on-air "confrontation" and "snit."

Alice is about the most gentle person I've ever met, so a confrontation and snit with Alice is not your ordinary confrontation and snit. Here is an excerpt.

Me: Were you aware that Angie Dickinson didn't want to talk about
   Frank Sinatra? (*Alice stares at me.*) You were not aware of that?
Alice: No. I had no idea.
Me: Because I was uncomfortable . . . a little bit, because she was uncomfortable . . . you had no idea, you just didn't know . . .
Alice: No, I didn't. I had no idea. I'm sorry.
Me: No, that's okay. I don't want you to be upset. You're not upset,
   are you?
Alice: No. No. Excuse me.
(*Alice walks away as I sit there looking distraught for offending her.*)

As I looked at the videos of these snits, the one with Alice was the only one I could watch without getting uncomfortable myself. Even though these were planned sketches they were still very edgy.

My encounter with my producer Clay Dettmer had to do with *New York* magazine. They had been talking about doing a major piece on the show for some time, and off camera I would sometimes ask Clay how that was going. That was the background for this confrontation and snit with Clay. Here we both do the confronting.

Me: Do they want to do a piece or not? What?

Clay: I feel like you're grinding me!

Me: No, I'm not grinding you.

Clay: It feels like the third degree.

Me: No, no, I don't mean it like a third degree. Do they want to do a piece is all I'm asking.

Clay: They want to do a piece. What do you want, a guarantee? I've been on the phone all day. It doesn't happen in a second like that!

Me (to camera): Y'know, it's so weird in all these years we've gotten along. I think the problem is if you keep the relationship off television, you're okay. The minute you take it on...(*To Clay:*) Have I offended you? Have I made you...

Clay: Why are you doing this to me on TV, Chuck? I don't get it.

Me (a deep sigh): I'm really not doing anything. I just want to know if *New York* magazine wants to do a piece or not.

Clay (angrily storming off the set): Let me go make a call! All right! I'm going to check it out!

Me: Yeah, make a call.

New York magazine, by the way, did eventually do a very long piece that was for the most part highly flattering. The title of the story was "Mr. Angry."

Another snit I did was with my daughter, Marion, who served the show as its field producer. Earlier, when I wanted to bring Marion onto the staff, Roger Ailes raised his eyebrows about as high as they could get, but whatever his feelings, Roger and, of course, Andy Friendly always supported me even when they were dubious. I just said, "Wait till you see her work." She's a very witty, charming lady who quickly became an audience favorite. Today she's a successful stand-up comedienne who also produces and MC's shows at the top comedy clubs in New York. I'll be very surprised if she doesn't one day soon host her own show on television.

Marion had been doing comic field pieces on the streets of New York in freezing winter weather, and off camera I was always worried if she was dressed warmly enough. That was the background for this excerpt from the snit.

Me: So just take care of yourself.

Marion: Okay. I do . . . Okay . . .

Me: I don't want to overstate it . . .

Marion: No, Dad . . . I do . . . I got it.

Me: Because you keep getting a cold.

Marion: I got it. I got it. I got it.

Me: I'm not saying you don't get it—

Marion: No, but I *really* got it.

Me: But you still go out there and do it, and you really don't dress warmly. . . .

Marion: No, I'm good . . . I'm telling you, I'm good.

Me: Yeah . . .

Marion: I just need to say that I'm good. I got it. I heard it. Okay?

Me: What do you mean by "You're good"?

Marion: No, I just feel a little suffocated. I understood it, okay? I got
   it. I don't...

Me: You understand what I'm saying?

Marion: Yeah.

Me: You're going to dress warmly?

Marion (storming off the set): Yeah, I said I... Okay!

Me: All right!

My producer, John Gabriel, booked the singers. John is also a
highly accomplished singer himself. In this segment John did both
the confronting and the snit. Here's an excerpt.

Me: Part of my appreciation of you is your understanding that you
   couldn't be a producer *and* be one of the singers yourself.

John: No, no, I wear different hats. I'm grateful for the opportunity,
   because this music is so underrepresented. We have rock, we
   have rap, we have country, but this kind of music you don't
   hear.

Me: And you've brought it to the show.

John: I must say, though, I do keep praying for a snowstorm.

Me: Uh... how do you mean, a snowstorm?

John: Well... if a singer's coming in and there's a snowstorm, and
   they can't make it... y'know... (*John looks at me expectantly.*)

Me (uncomfortably): Yeah... uh... see, your function as a producer is
   paramount here. You are primarily a producer.

John (interrupting): No, no, no. It's the format. You need a singer
   every night. That's the way the show is structured, and I would
   be delighted to fill that position, if somebody can't make it. I
   mean, if there's an emergency.

Me: And you *could* fill that position beautifully, but I wouldn't want...I mean...we...we...I...

John (jumping in): No, wait, Charlie, are you telling me if we had a singer and they couldn't make it, and I'm here, that you wouldn't say, "John, go on and sing"?

Me: Well...

John: I can't *believe* this!

Me: No, I mean...none of the producers on the shows on CNBC appear as singers.

John: But they're not singers! I am a *singer*!

Me (looking increasingly uncomfortable): No, I know...I know...I guess we need to hold that you are a producer, and if a singer couldn't come, I guess we would just—

John: You don't like the way I sing!

Me: No, I love the way, I love the way, y'know I'm your biggest fan, but I think even if there was a snowstorm, and the singer couldn't come....

John: Really?

Me: Well...

John: I gotta tell you I'm offended.

Me (squirming): Aw...don't...

John: I'm offended by that.

Me: Oh, please don't be offended, don't be offended. No. It's not personal.

John (astonished): How can it not be personal, Charlie? I'm a singer, and I'm here, and a singer doesn't show up, and you don't say, "John, please sing"? No, I understand very clearly. Thank you very much!

(John gets up and walks off the set.)

Someone who had known John and me for a long time saw this and absolutely believed it was real.

I guess if we had been on Comedy Central, people would have known it was a joke. Since the show often dealt with serious issues, it's easy to see how people wouldn't be sure. Today I see that as both an asset and a flaw.

The most extreme practitioner of the comedy of discomfort I ever saw was Andy Kaufman.

I was at Town Hall in New York when Andy did a show there relatively early in his career. For those of you not familiar with what Andy did, he would first appear as "Tony Clifton." Tony was a stunningly hostile lounge singer with a big bad hairpiece, who very quickly, after showing off a less than mediocre voice, began to assault the audience. I got the impression a sizable portion of the crowd had no idea that this was, in fact, Andy. They began to scream at him to get off the stage, as they wanted to see Andy. Tony Clifton just screamed back at them with more venom. If you were there, no matter what you might have thought about it, again, it wasn't dull.

A few weeks later, I spent a little time with Andy. I suggested he bring Tony Clifton on later in the evening, to let more people in on the joke. Andy just looked at me and said, "Tony's my opening act." I stared at him a moment and decided not to pursue it any further.

I met Andy when I was hanging around for a time with the *Saturday Night Live* crowd in the late 1970s. I hosted the show in '77 and chose to do something that again was in the comedy-of-discomfort area. My idea was to act as though I'd realized just before air time that the show was live. The script indicated that I'd missed most of the rehearsals, as I was busy catching Broadway shows and buying gifts for the cast. When I did the Samurai sketch with John Belushi, I just kept commenting on John's extraordinary makeup. I basically stopped each scene, as though I were really enthralled with what everyone was doing. There was plenty of mail from people bitterly complaining about me ruining the show, and I'm told about an equal amount from people who enjoyed it.

Later I was asked to host again, but I chose not to. I can either learn a script or improvise, but neither was really possible there. The script changed right up until air time, forcing you to read the TelePrompTers, and you certainly couldn't improvise, because the show is done to fit ninety minutes—live. Most hosts I've observed seem to handle it fine.

Easily one of the most uncomfortable people I ran into there was John Belushi, who also made plenty of others uneasy. I always found it ironic that John approached Carol Burnett and me separately about being involved in the Friendly movement, because he personally felt he was not treated with enough friendliness.

When I sang "The Sounds of Silence" wearing an Art Garfunkel wig with my musical guest Paul Simon, I acted as though I didn't know the words, causing Paul to finally walk off in "exasperation."

Again, about equal amounts of people were irritated and amused.

Bill Murray was just beginning, the season I hosted *Saturday Night Live*. I remember being impressed with him and offering to try to get him an agent. In a bee sketch where we appeared together, as the bees exited in "disgust" after I spent the scene telling them their moving antennas were distracting, Bill ad-libbed the word *parasite* at me. Later he came over to make sure I wasn't offended. He wasn't kidding either. When you work in the arena of discomfort, offended would be the last thing you should be.

A Loaded Situation

Having a talk show obviously can put you into conversation with people from another time of your life who under normal circumstances you would probably never see again, and sometimes the situation is loaded. This was the case when my first New York acting teacher, the legendary teacher and actress Uta Hagen, was booked. I don't believe I had seen her in about thirty-five years, but I knew she had been aware of me for more than one reason.

When I was a kid I had some unusual relationships with a couple of teachers, and it was always for the same reason: I bothered them because they thought I asked too many questions. It's good I finally found a field where there wasn't such a thing as too many questions, but when I was around eleven in Hebrew school, I had an extraordinary experience. The problem came because the Hebrew teacher had us repeating Hebrew sentences after him for what seemed like a very long time. Having probably a below-average threshold for that kind of thing, I asked, "What is it we're saying?" The teacher ignored me, which just provoked me to ask again. (I'm someone who incidentally never thought Sam Donaldson went too far.) When I persisted in trying to determine what we were saying, he told me to leave. I don't know if he meant for that day or for good, but I left for good. It was kind of a "you can't fire me, I quit" situation. Later I hooked up with another teacher, Rabbi Morris Kaplan, who was magnificent and delighted in answering any questions. He even called me "Sonny"!

In high school, I irritated my economics teacher, Mr. Kennedy, because I just couldn't follow some of his points, and kept asking questions. Being pretty much an *A* student, I was even arrogant enough to say, "If I don't understand this, maybe some other kids might not either." He regularly threw me out of class and told me to go to the principal's office. I was the class president (forgive me for saying *A* student and class president in the same paragraph, but I think it's a clearer story if you know that). The principal would say to me, "I never know if you're here for class business, or if you've just been thrown out of class again."

I really hadn't changed at all by the time Uta Hagen accepted me into her acting class after an audition. Even though she was a famous actress and teacher, and I was a twenty-one-year-old student, I felt it was completely appropriate to question what we were doing. We were spending a whole lot of time on exercises that had us carrying imaginary suitcases and opening imaginary windows, and I didn't really get it. You could say we were developing our imaginations, but honestly, then and now, I didn't really get *that* much emphasis on the suitcases and windows. So I asked.

The Hebrew teacher and the economics teacher had nothing on Uta Hagen! She really resented the question, especially since I found ways to ask more than once. Uta is a highly intelligent and charming woman but she easily expressed her frustration and dislike of me. She even threatened to throw me out of class a few times, but never did. There must have been something about the way I received her attacks, because after a while the situation turned. Eventually I would actually sit behind her and give her a shoulder rub, and she would say things like, "This kid questions everything, which is, I guess, the way it should be." By the time I left after three years, we were on warm terms. However, twenty-five years later when I wrote my first book and again expressed my opinion of the imaginary suitcases and the imaginary windows, I heard she didn't appreciate it.

So here we were, thirty-five years later, and she's my guest on my television show. I really didn't know what to expect. Happily, she greeted me warmly, and as I recall, quickly made some reference to the suitcases and windows by saying, "There was a lot more going on than that." In fairness, there absolutely was. Uta then implied that at this point she too wouldn't rate carrying imaginary suitcases and raising imaginary windows at the top of her list of most important acting lessons. I think the real reason she warmed to me was that whenever asked, I contributed over the years to her school. There was a good reason for that. When I was studying, Uta and her husband, Herbert Berghof, kept the price per class at three dollars. It was one of the most highly regarded schools in New York, and it had to be the least expensive. That's something this former penniless actor never forgot.

I recently encountered Uta at a Christmas party. I quickly sat next to her on the sofa. Already sitting there was an old friend of mine who knew Uta as well. Both Uta and I addressed some of our remarks to this fellow in an attempt to keep the exchange from getting too heavy for a party. The subject quickly came around to the imaginary suitcases and windows. Uta said to me, "I've been waiting years to really tell you off." She then turned to our mutual friend and said, "He came into my class like a know-it-all and tried to tell me what to do." All this was said with a half smile from Uta. I went to a two-thirds smile, and said that I wasn't even like that today, let alone as a beginning student of twenty-one, but if I had offended her, I was terribly sorry. She seemed taken aback to get such a genuine apology from an alleged wise guy and quickly gave me a kiss. All's well that ends well.

Blowups

The concept of having singers singing my favorite standards at the end of every show was applauded by many people. It also was an idea that illustrated how naive I was about the realities of television.

It became apparent after a while that the singers, probably the most popular part of the show for some viewers, were the least popular for others. It depended on your age. If these oldies but goodies brought back memories of your youth, then it was a golden time on the show. If, however, they were before your time, you tuned out. When about three months into the show I became aware of ratings, it was obvious that when we had the singers on, the ratings dropped. Still, no one said, "Get rid of the singers." Maybe it was because Roger Ailes and Andy Friendly enjoyed them as much as I did. Eventually, the question came: Does Chuck have to have singers every night? Then: How about just having them when you can get Rosemary Clooney or Jack Jones, etc.? I thought I was being treated very fairly. There was a recognition that the singers were a valuable asset, even if they didn't draw the largest audience.

CNBC was building its subscription base, and was realizing more revenue from that than advertising dollars, which are directly tied to ratings. After some time the ad money was growing in importance, and eventually it didn't seem in the interest of the long-term life of the show to continue with the singers. No one ever said, "Get rid of the singers," but it was too obvious to ignore. The same became true of the one-guest-per-show concept. You could sustain audience interest for a whole hour with very few people, so eventually two or three or more guests were booked for each show, and none of them sang.

While there were many wonderful singers who appeared, my single most vivid memory is unfortunately not a good one. Being in show business my whole life, I've always heard about temperamental actors. The only thing worse than that was supposed to be temperamental singers.

At the time of what I'm about to describe, we were taping some of our shows, and this singer appeared for an afternoon taping of a program that would be aired that night at ten. He ran a sound check prior to the taping, which all the singers did. When the time came to tape the song, he did something none of the singers did. He blew up! This wasn't right, and that wasn't right, there was feedback that had to be fixed, and during all of this he grew increasingly furious. He began to scream not only at the people in the booth but at anyone in sight, questioning whether different people had graduated college. We all sat there stunned. Rage seems to command quiet from everyone—at least for a while. Finally, he turned to me and bellowed, "How would you like your pants to fall down in front of a million people?" I just looked at him, choosing not to say that the audience wasn't anywhere near a million or, more important, that we were on tape, which he absolutely knew, and nobody's pants would fall down in front of anyone. Clearly, we were dealing with some form of neurosis, and we waited for it to pass, which it did. After a while, he sang his song just fine and that was that.

I promised everyone they'd never see him again, and they never did. A few days later he phoned me to ask if I could recommend a therapist. He probably knew more therapists than I did, but I guess it was his way of saying he was sorry. I particularly regretted that it happened, because I knew this man to be capable of wonderful kindness. Sad, the price some people have to pay to perform.

It's been widely reported that the late Helen Hayes, who was known as the first lady of the American theater, used to throw up from nerves before every performance. I hope for that nice lady's sake that's an exaggeration, but obviously every performer experiences anxiety to varying degrees.

Naturally that heart-pounding thing happens the loudest when you're starting out. In my early twenties I was on the television soap opera *Love of Life,* which was broadcast live. I remember being in a scene where I knocked on a door. After I finished knocking, my heart was pounding so loud that to my ear it was as though I was still knocking. When the person opened the door, the organist in the studio hit what was to me a surprise *da-dum* that made my heart feel like it was going to jump right through my chest.

Over the years, with experience, of course, nerves get better, but never completely go away. That's why I always tell people around performers to treat them as patients about to go into surgery: "Can I get you anything? Want me to rub your shoulders?"

Only once in my life did I hear someone criticized for too much kindness. A comedian friend of mine actually criticized his wife for laughing too hard at his jokes, which just goes to show you there really is an exception to every rule.

The first time I saw a blowup, it came not from a singer or an actor. It was the producer of a musical I directed off-Broadway in the 1960s. He had been trying to get me to fire the choreographer for some time prior to the opening, which I had refused to do. I had no idea what his problem with her was—something about more "crispness." The choreographer had more experience than all of us put together, and I thought it was ridiculous even to consider firing her. We were selling out in previews, and the audience clearly loved the show. Finally, he threatened to fire her himself, before the show opened. I told him if he tried that, I could stop him, as I was also the coauthor. I didn't really know what the legality of it all was, but the initially civilized going back and forth finally climaxed with him screaming at me in the lobby after a preview performance. He basically said I was nuts, and I pointed out he was the one screaming in public with his young boy watching. That only enraged him more. Also, he was late in paying the costume designer, who in retaliation stole all the costumes on opening night, causing the police to be called and delaying the opening for thirty minutes, which seemed like forever. It was certainly enough to alienate some of the audience. It still got a number of rave reviews, and by the way, the choreographer was widely praised. It didn't run very long, though, because the *New York Times* critic didn't like it. In fairness, I don't think the *Times* critic would have liked it even if the curtain had gone up on time.

Most of the behavior I've seen over the years that I wish I hadn't seen did come from actors and actresses. An actor in a Broadway show I directed was unhappy with an actress he was playing opposite. He wasn't the kind of man who would confront people in life, so in the middle of a scene in which they were arguing, he pulled a gun (definitely not in the script!). I was watching from the back of the theater. The audience didn't believe it was a real gun (it wasn't), although you certainly couldn't tell from where I was standing. I went backstage immediately with a few choice words. He had no explanation, of course. How could he? He just left the company as soon as his contract allowed. Looking back, I can't believe I didn't fire him on the spot.

Then there was the actress I directed in a play I wrote and was trying out in a summer theater. There was no budget, so the cast was asked to supply their own clothes. All this woman was required to come up with was a nice dress. She showed up for rehearsal with a dress that was covered with something that reflected light in every direction. When I asked her to come up with a plainer dress, she claimed that was all she had. "Everything else is too small," she said. I offered to buy her something more appropriate, but she said there was no time. I stopped talking then, because I realized that whatever I'd say, she'd have a comeback. After I stopped playing her crazy game, she said, "So what do you want me to do?" I said, "I don't know. I've suggested everything I can." Somehow, at the opening, she came up with a perfectly fine dress.

I worked with an actress in a movie who called me before we began filming to tell me she didn't think she was very good and was really counting on my help. When she showed up to work, she barely spoke to me or anyone else. I had never before or since met anyone that cold. I later heard she was having trouble in her relationship with her boyfriend. Of course, if everyone who had trouble in a relationship acted that way, the whole world would feel like the Arctic Circle.

This actress once complained that I had all the lines in a scene, so I said, "Would you like to say them?" She seemed surprised by the offer and with the director's approval took them as though they were a hot fudge sundae. In fact, it was just a lot of necessary plot information that no actor of experience would relish saying. When she saw the scene in the screening room the next day, she acted as though I had put one over on her. (Maybe I had.)

Then there was the actor who felt I had pulled a fast one on him. I was never crazy about doing behind-the-scenes interviews in movies. To hear an actor talk about his character, for me, is not only uninteresting but really counterproductive to the illusion you're trying to create. When I see behind-the-scenes documentaries on how special effects work, it's even worse.

I made my feelings about these interviews known to a male co-star in a movie. The producers asked me to do the interview, and I said I would, even though I'd prefer not to. This actor assumed, given my attitude, I would do something perfunctory, which, no matter how I felt, I would never do.

A few days later he stormed into a room to confront me. He said the producers had just told him I was really funny in my interview, and he wasn't, and would he like to try again?

He thought I had set him up by saying I didn't like to do these interviews, so I'd be funny, and he wouldn't. I pointed out that contrary to what he thought, it was in my absolute interest that he be funny, because if he wasn't, it wasn't likely the movie would be a success. This poor guy consistently thought people were out to do him in, and never seemed to know all these plots were in his head.

The most paranoid person I ever met was an actor I did a play with several years ago.

This guy was enraged because he felt somehow that what I was doing on stage implied he was gay. He asked me to come into his dressing room, where he circled me in a fury. I just stood there staring at him as he vented his rage. When he seemed to be worn out, I quietly and in a very friendly way told him I had no idea what he was talking about.

I guess he believed me, because he seemed all right after that, and also I'm sure it wasn't the first time he blew up at someone who looked at him with the same baffled look I had.

It's so sad what some people carry with them all through their lives.

The oddest bad behavior I ever witnessed came from a fella I had worked with whom I raved about in print. This guy was deeply offended that I didn't say even more about him.

Then there was the actress I worked with in a play who came up with the most extraordinary suggestion for the director, who disagreed with her on a script point. The director had said, "Even though I'm not a woman, I believe I can understand the psychology of this female character." The actress responded, "Every time a male director suggests to me he understands my character better than I do, I feel like telling him to cut off his penis and swallow it." The director, the playwright, and I got very interested in the paint on the ceiling for a few moments, until we all got interested in the texture of the rug, waiting for those words to no longer be hanging in the air.

Alan Dershowitz
and O. J. Simpson

The real turn in what I was doing on television came with the O. J. Simpson case. My involvement with that a few months after I went on the air led to looking at the justice system as a whole, as well as other political and social issues.

The degree of incriminating evidence in the Simpson case astonished me, beginning with people's blood in places it shouldn't have been. I always felt that if this man was going to be found not guilty, then they should open the prisons and let a whole lot of people out, because thousands have been convicted on less evidence than was presented here. As with everything else that came up over that five-year period, I made no secret of my feelings. When Alan Dershowitz appeared on my program, he snapped at me, "You're the problem. You make up your mind before all the evidence is in!" I snapped back with something like, "No, you're the problem. You and all these defense attorneys talking in circles and nobody has any idea what you're talking about!" Alan's charge of my making up my mind too easily really was ironic. Many people speculated that Alan was quickly added to the defense team after public appearances where he said, in effect, if the case ever went to trial, it wouldn't be a question of whether O. J. Simpson committed the murders but what mitigating circumstances there might be. In other words, Alan Dershowitz seemed to have made up his mind about who did it before all the evidence was in.

Over the years, I have found myself in agreement with Alan on most issues, but on the Simpson case we were at each other for months. This all culminated in a live ninety-minute debate moderated by Geraldo Rivera.

Alan was on the satellite, and he insisted Geraldo and I not share the same studio, thinking it would give me an unfair advantage. So even though Geraldo and I were in the same building, we were in separate studios. Alan was probably right to want that, because during the commercial breaks I marched over to Geraldo's studio and yelled, "Get him to answer the damn questions!"

There were lawyers around CNBC who found it astonishing that I was going to debate a renowned Harvard law professor on a court case. I had no trepidation at all about it, for two reasons. First, I had a strong position to argue, and second, I knew from my previous encounters with Alan that he would make a lot of technical legal points that people would perceive as not only irrelevant but too esoteric for debate purposes.

Here's an example. He claimed that Mark Fuhrman could have selectively answered questions on the stand after he took the Fifth. Specifically, he said Fuhrman could have answered the question on whether he planted evidence or not. He cited a ruling from the Illinois Court of Appeals to make his point. I countered with, "Do you think Fuhrman felt he could selectively answer questions?" He said his lawyer certainly knew he could. Alan claimed to conclude that Fuhrman didn't want to answer the question on planting evidence. This was absurd, because he had already answered it on television appearances, including with me. Obviously if the defense had proof he'd planted evidence, we would have long since heard it. As far as legally whether he could have selectively answered questions, I'm not a lawyer, but I know in this instance, lawyers will disagree.

Fuhrman had been my guest on a couple of shows. I took the wildly unpopular position of defending him. There were several reasons for this. Clearly, someone can do something wrong and not be compared to Hitler, as he was. What exactly did he do? Obviously he lied about using the *N* word, but there's a big jump from that to Hitler. Not only is there no indication he planted evidence, there is more than ample proof he did not. There were more than a dozen officers scouring the murder scene before Fuhrman arrived, and no one saw a glove that Fuhrman, according to Johnnie Cochran, saw and transplanted to Simpson's house. If that glove was the only piece of evidence, it might be one thing, but since you have Simpson's blood at the murder scene and Nicole and Ron's blood in Simpson's Bronco—give me a break.

The attacks on Alan that poured into CNBC were by far the greatest in number and venom on anyone who ever appeared. Just as with myself, I chose not to read the criticism of Alan. One strange comment did get through to me, however. Someone called him "a Hitler hater."

As far as listening to lawyers on television talk about their cases, here's a quote from the August 9, 1982, issue of *U.S. News & World Report* on defense attorneys: "The defendant wants to hide the truth, because he's generally guilty. The defense attorney's job is to make sure the jury does not arrive at that truth." The quote is from Alan Dershowitz. As far as the O. J. Simpson case goes, personally I have no doubt Alan believes Simpson is guilty.

This reminds me of when I had Thomas Puccio as a guest. He was the defense attorney for the now-convicted rapist Alex Kelly. Puccio not only wanted us to believe, before the case was decided, that his client wasn't a rapist, but implied you should be perfectly comfortable if Mr. Kelly volunteered to baby-sit your teenage daughter. It seems that for years now, young women have been popping up with horror stories about Mr. Kelly, but of course, there was Puccio, close to nominating his client for choir boy of the year. We should never lose the awareness that that's what defense attorneys may do.

Belatedly, it became clear to Alan that having a public debate with someone over a period of months who has his own television show is not a good idea, especially since Alan was on the side of someone who the public overwhelmingly believes is a double murderer.

For those of you who may have been persuaded by Simpson's protestations of innocence all these years, think of Susan Smith's "sincerity" as she pleaded for the kidnapper to return her two children, whom she later admitted to drowning.

The response to the Dershowitz debate that poured into the network not surprisingly had me (or I should say my side) winning 85 percent to 15 percent. I don't think it helped Alan that he chose to smile throughout the debate with me, I guess in an effort to appear charming. I'm sure he can be, but to most people it's really tough to defend O. J. Simpson and be charming at the same time.

In retrospect, I do think Alan was right, however, in charging me with using my television show as a venue to go after him more than was reasonable. I didn't see it at the time, but now I think it was inappropriate.

I also believe that at times, during my coverage of the Simpson trial, I allowed myself to become too emotional on the air. This really increased the polarization with people who saw things differently. That was a mistake.

Unfortunately, there is anger and resentment all over television. I understand it, but it only further divides us.

The moment I'm proudest of in my coverage of the trial came when I opened a live show and without comment put on a pair of surgical gloves. I then attempted to put a pair of regular gloves I had bought that absolutely fit me over them. I really struggled to get them on. Then I took off the surgical gloves and easily put the gloves on. When the gloves didn't fit Simpson, he, of course, had on surgical gloves. After that, on air demonstrations during trials were banned at CNBC.

Maybe the weirdest moment in the whole Simpson saga came for me in the civil trial when the defense presented an expert of some kind, and his name was Grodin!

Later, somebody sent me a radio tape on which Alan is heard saying he would defend Hitler. I asked his friend Elie Wiesel about that in a later interview, and Elie said he was sure Alan wasn't serious. Alan, of course, was serious, and for me that is the bravest thing about Alan Dershowitz and the most foolish. He stands behind the necessary credo that everyone is entitled to an attorney, but of course, nowhere does it say everyone is entitled to *him* as an attorney. Being willing to represent O. J. Simpson or Adolf Hitler leaves Alan vulnerable to the ongoing charge that he craves the spotlight. It also undermines whatever worthy causes he does champion, because he creates so much ill will from every quarter.

Since Alan does so much pro bono work, I suggested to a friend of mine from Amnesty International who was trying to get strong representation for a prisoner on death row that she contact Alan. She said there was so much negative feeling toward him, he could do more harm than good.

None of this should take away from Alan's brilliance, so, of course, when all is said and done, I'm glad there is an Alan Dershowitz. He speaks eloquently on behalf of oppressed people. Mostly we are on the same side, and my encounters with him moved me out of the "dessert" category and into the position of someone who speaks out on issues. Unintentionally, he became a great benefactor to me.

Howard Stern and *Saturday Night Live* and Rush Limbaugh

Another unintentional benefactor was Howard Stern. Someone sent me a video of him "having fun" with the remains of a young woman who had died of a drug overdose. He played with her bones that remained after cremation. He offered "to glue her together." He told her boyfriend who had brought the remains to chew pieces of bone fragments. He picked up a piece of bone and said, "Look at the size of this! That looks like a piece of her head." He later had to pay for emotional distress caused her family in an out-of-court settlement.

He also found it humorous to do sound effects of a plane crashing when John Denver was killed, and played gunshots when the singer Selena was murdered.

Is this terminal detachment? Arrested development?

Here's a man in his forties who is obsessed with looking at women's breasts and speculating on who's a real blonde or redhead. A sexually retarded adult who doesn't even seem to know it. It's sad that such a person enjoys such a large following and the friendship of otherwise estimable people. It's another example of money and power corrupting values. I used the video of him having fun with the remains over and over again. Again, the FCC prohibits certain kinds of broadcasting from 6 A.M. to 10 P.M. to protect children. Many of us feel Stern has violated this for years. He's paid plenty of fines, but there he is, year after year, still spewing his garbage. He often reminds me of the Lenny Bruce line, "The reason novelty stores started selling plastic puke is they did so well with the s—."

People in the media who deplore Stern are very careful not to attack him publicly, fearing his unending retaliatory wrath. I had no such fear, for one reason. While I knew it would be there, I also knew I'd never hear it, because everyone who comes into contact with me knows not to deliver negative news. So while Stern would always hear whatever I would say about him, I would never hear what he had to say about me. If you ever meet either of us, you'll notice one of us seems happy and the other not so happy. I figured out a long time ago that listening to destructive comments is— guess what—destructive.

On a more personal note, I will never forget how Stern reduced my friend the late Gilda Radner to tears after badgering her with questions about her sex life.

In any case, Stern, like Dershowitz, unintentionally was a boost to me. I heard it from several people, so I benefited from taking him on, and I didn't suffer at all from the abuse, because I never heard it.

The desire to shock often takes talented people into strange places.

Years ago, I was hanging around with some producers at *Saturday Night Live* when they were in a battle with the network over whether they'd be allowed to do a comedy sketch where the characters would be the Charles Manson women. I asked them why they wanted to do that. Of course, the subject is about as funny as the Holocaust.

Their focus seemed to be more on winning the freedom to do whatever they wanted, to be as outrageous and shocking as they wanted to be. To this day, I find it hard to believe they thought it was funny.

Michael O'Donoghue, one of their writers and performers, pretended to stick big needles in his eyes, then collapsed and writhed in mock agony on the floor. I knew Michael, who died in 1994. I don't believe he found that funny. Shocking? Sure.

So what we're really talking about here is the desire to shock. To be in really horrific taste and to shock is the goal. To me that's worse than sophomoric. It's untalented sophomoric, and what's really a shame is that the people doing all this usually have plenty of authentic talent. They obviously don't need this to be successful. I felt the brilliant *Saturday Night Live* people should consider the Manson idea beneath them, as a pie in the face would be for "hipper, fresher" humor.

I don't remember if they got to show it or not, but I did give an interview a year or so later, and said pretty much what I've said here about some of the things they've done, and word got back to me that people at *SNL* were offended I'd criticize them. I understand that, but I believe even friends and colleagues have to be honest when asked a question.

I believe I also benefited from the venom of Rush Limbaugh, or one of his listeners he quoted, saying something like he wished Geraldo, Dershowitz, and I would get strokes while speaking on the air. Limbaugh didn't personally call for the strokes, just added that he could "understand" the listener's feeling. This hatred came over what they felt was our defense of President Clinton during the impeachment proceedings. I am, of course, less familiar with Geraldo's and Alan's sentiments than my own, but my "defense" was simply that the president's actions were not "high crimes" calling for removal from office. Personally, I have never been able to feel the same about President Clinton since his indulgence, but I prefer him by far to his "hater" adversaries. To me, anyone as sexually driven as the president has an emotional problem that is so destructive to himself and others that he is to be pitied, not hated. Yet hate is what I so often hear when I make an attempt to listen to Limbaugh and others of his ilk every few months. I usually last less than about five minutes, as he and his callers struggle for the words to express their vitriol. It's stunning to me. I've never heard a civilized "agree to disagree." These people are so blinded by their biases that they can see only demons on the other side. This attitude, of course, is perpetuated by Mr. Limbaugh. How can one point of view be so right and the other so wrong? Is it possible that the other side of your political agenda has absolutely nothing valid for you even to consider? Of course not. What does it say about you if you can never ever see anything of merit in another person's argument? You would enjoy more respect and credibility if you acknowledge that all good does not reside on your side and all bad on the other. Also, for callers to dominate the air waves to express hatred rather than to put forth ideas on how to help people is deeply troubling.

The other day I was scanning the radio dial and I heard Rush Limbaugh doing a promo for his program. He was challenging the media to stake out Bill Clinton's Harlem office to report exactly how much time he spends there. I'm not exactly sure what his point was, since the ex-president had been out of office for some time.

Republican congressional whip Dick Armey is another benefactor of mine who was quoted as saying, on my being canceled from CNBC, "Thank the Lord. Thank the Lord twice." He was silent when I was back on MSNBC within a month. We called his office to hear exactly what about me upset the congressman so much, but got no response.

The rebuttal to such people can never be as strong as the cost to themselves of their own hatred.

Being Attacked

Former Senator Alan Simpson of Wyoming was a guest on the show one night along with my friend Jonathan Alter of NBC News and *Newsweek*. Under discussion was the Food Lion suit against ABC for having its employees falsely identify themselves in order to be hired by Food Lion, where they revealed practices such as "painting" meat that was not fresh and changing expiration dates on food. Food Lion didn't deny the accusations but sued ABC for false representation on its employees' applications. Food Lion won the case and was awarded millions, but fortunately the award was overturned on appeal, and Food Lion got about eight bucks or so. Senator Simpson was passionately against any falsification by the media to gain access under any circumstances, and Jon Alter and I were just as passionate in feeling sometimes that was the only way to uncover the cheats, crooks, and even killers among us who will do anything to you to make money for themselves. At one point, the senator snapped at me, "There you go, putting on your Jesus shoes!"

At the end of the interview, Senator Simpson complained bitterly that it was two (Jon Alter and I) against one (the senator). "Next time make it two on two, and make it an even fight!" Maybe that was a fair criticism, but I honestly felt that a United States senator should be more than capable of handling an extremely smart journalist and the not-that-long-ago co-star of the *Beethoven* movies.

I always shake my head when I hear that a person must be willing to take criticism. Of course you must take criticism from the people in charge. The problem is, people everywhere are always ready to offer criticism, and it's difficult for me to remember many people who gave it with any awareness that they might be wrong. I have found much of the criticism (with obvious notable exceptions from extremely bright, sensitive people) to be not constructive but destructive. Really sharp people suggest something different rather than tear down what they see. A destructive director I once had on a movie said to me, "You're coming off funereal," instead of just asking for more energy.

The producer of that movie told me the director had said he'd happily listen to anything the producer had to say, as long as he didn't approach him on the set.

One day after the filming was completed, the producer approached the director and made a comment about an incredibly violent shoot-out the director had filmed. The producer's point was that so much violence would have attracted significant police presence. The director blew up, screaming, "That's the best g—damn shoot-out I've ever done!"

Once this director came to a party for the cast with a prostitute he'd hired and suggestively danced with her while holding a bottle of whiskey in his hand. I think he thought he was *in* a movie rather than directing one.

I remember a critic saying of a movie I wrote, "If you want to know what it feels like to die sitting upright in your seat, go see this movie." Another critic said of the same movie, "You'll laugh till you cry." Neither was true. The point is, it's all pretty subjective, and it certainly doesn't do me any good to think I'm killing people sitting upright in their movie seats. Another time a critic said of one of my acting appearances, "It would be sad to think an acting career lay ahead." The next year I won a best actor award on Broadway.

I have been told I talk too much, and I have been told I talk too little with equal certainty. I have been told I must do more comedy, and I have been told it's way more important I stay serious. Again, each person speaking seemingly would stake his or her life, or certainly reputation, on those words. Most people simply fail to see how subjective everything is

I ran into Joan Rivers at an event recently, and we were talking about this. Joan said she was headlining in a big room in Las Vegas, and an old school chum saw her show, and told her why this or that didn't work. Amazing. People who have had lifetime careers in this most precarious of professions probably know a little bit more about what works for them than someone passing through, wouldn't you say?

I do, however, particularly remember a constructive criticism I received from the famed acting coach Mira Rostova, who was a friend of mine. I remember it because to this day, over twenty-five years later, it resonates importantly for life itself.

I was in the play *Same Time, Next Year* on Broadway. Mira came to see me and called my attention to a moment when the female character, played by the magnificent Ellen Burstyn, tells my character that she was up sick in the night. I say, "I didn't hear you." Mira pointed out that I said it as though I didn't believe her, and asked if that was my intention. I said it absolutely wasn't. I was completely unaware that it sounded that way, but as soon as she called it to my attention, it was easy to see, and I made the adjustment. I still think of this today, because more and more over the years I see that lack of awareness is at the heart of so many problems in life.

If every criticism had the enormous value of Mira Rostova's observation over a quarter of a century ago, I'd be running up and down the street asking people, "What do you think?" instead of having an unlisted number.

Meanwhile, things were just sailing along at CNBC. I was alternating O. J. Simpson shows with more and more shows on social issues—homelessness, hunger, domestic violence, and prison reform.

I had no idea that behind the scenes, meetings were taking place at NBC that would soon radically change the whole situation.

Advocacy

It was Bill Bolster, one of the executives at CNBC who arrived after I did, who once asked, "How did that communist ever get his own talk show in the first place?"

The perception of me as a left-wing commentator is a good example of why labels don't work.

The subject of politics never came up when I was hired by Roger Ailes at CNBC. Roger, who now heads the Fox News Channel, is a well-known conservative who once was a key figure in the senior George Bush's successful campaign for president. He also, as I've said, is a friend of mine. Politics never came up when we met, because I was a comedy actor who was hired to provide "dessert" after Geraldo Again, the serious side emerged with the O. J. Simpson trial and my battles with Alan Dershowitz, which led the show toward weighty issues.

When it did turn in that direction, my close friend of thirty-five years and then producer, John Gabriel, would sit off camera and stare at me show after show. The reason for that was, as John put it, "I've known him for thirty-five years, we were even roommates at one point, and not only did I never hear him talk about any of this, I had no idea he knew all this stuff!" Other friends said the same, and it was true. Another friend asked, "Are you really as passionate on all these issues as you seem to be on television?" The question clearly seemed to suggest I wasn't, but I never took offense, because I understood why it was raised. If you had hung around with me through most of my life, you would not have heard me talking about social issues. The exceptions were the Simon and Garfunkel special and the Friendly movement, and even then the expressions were all on television, rarely in a social context.

The truth is, my feelings are so strong on a number of issues that if I did talk about them in a social situation, before too long it wouldn't be much of a social situation. Have you ever discussed abortion in a social situation? Well, it could get like that with me on several subjects.

Three recent instances come to mind.

My wife and I had dinner with some conservative friends we've known for years. The conversation after dinner turned toward the killings of some unarmed black men by the police in New York City.

Our conservative friends had invited other conservative friends to the dinner, and as the discussion went on, it somehow turned to sentiments like, "I have no particular sympathy for blacks," etc.

For the moment, I held my tongue and stared into my fruit cup. It was a party!

Finally the hostess, of all people, whom I know to be a bright, sensitive, lovely person, looked at me and said, "Chuck, you must have something to say on this."

I hope I responded very respectfully, but the party ended shortly after that.

Then there was the time the Bronx "Baby Bombers" were representing New York for the national championship in Little League baseball.

I had some people over to my house, and one of the guys, whom I love, said, "It's hard for me to root for them. They all speak Spanish."

The party didn't end when I commented on his comment, but it clearly slowed down.

When it was later revealed that the star pitcher was two years older than was allowed, that troubled me as much as anyone. I've seen unfair competition too often in youth sports.

Of course, some people feel it's done so often they don't even see anything wrong with it. They say, "Everybody does it." I can imagine speaking up in one of those groups and ending a party there as well.

At another gathering where I was a guest, someone suggested we go around the table and give our feelings about Gary Condit and Chandra Levy.

Because most likely a young woman was murdered, I didn't feel that was a subject for a party game, and when it came my turn to talk I said that. Again, the party didn't end, but it slowed measurably.

I have some conservative friends who perceived me as an extremist. I would always counter by saying there was not one subject that I talk about where they held the opposite position. To prove my point, I would ask these questions:

1. Was there anyone who *wanted* children to go to bed hungry?

2. Was there anyone who didn't care that homeless people would freeze to death on the streets of our cities in the winter?

3. Do you really think it's okay to lock up mothers of small children for twenty years for selling two ounces of cocaine for the first time? (Then I would add they often were addicts or set up and entrapped by the police.)

So it really wasn't what I stood for that got to people as much as the intensity and the amount of time I talked about it on the air. I believe I focus on all of this because I grew up in a household where fairness and a sense of right and wrong were front and center.

I vividly remember an incident when I was about twelve years old. My dad had a teenage black kid working for him who was arrested, but while he was out on bail he continued in his job. When I asked my dad about it, he said, "He was arrested but hadn't yet been found guilty."

There were almost no black people in our area, and my dad's response was certainly not a given, so it had a strong effect on me.

My mother and older brother, Jack, were excellent role models as well. There wasn't a lot of conversation about all of this. Things just were a certain way, and that way simply was to care about other people, also not to spend time putting others down.

Since I was perceived so much as a left-wing guy, it always confused people when I seemed to have positions closely associated with the right. I personally would want nothing to do with abortion, even though I'd be against a law to outlaw it, because experience tells us people would find a way to get it done in probably more dangerous ways. As a left winger, I shouldn't be talking so much against the free speech of Howard Stern, but clearly, in my opinion, the time of day he broadcasts puts him in violation of laws. I am also pretty strongly a "family values" person, a concept most identify with conservatism.

I am against capital punishment for every reason you can imagine, not the least of which is that overwhelmingly it is the poor and people of color who are executed. Also, there is no doubt in my mind that innocent people have been, and will continue to be, killed by the state, because of mistaken eyewitness identification and faulty lab work, among other reasons. That's considered a left-wing position, but I read in the papers today that the very conservative Reverend Pat Robertson has embraced it. Labeling people is not a good idea. It's just too superficial a way to look at things.

I once had a friendly debate with a well-known conservative friend off the air. He began by saying to me, "You think big government programs are the solution to everything." I said I had no idea what the solutions were to our problems. People more qualified than I should address that. I just identified our problems differently than some. I urged we focus more on the unprotected people.

He said if he were mayor of a town, he would have every family of wealth "adopt" five poor families and look after them.

It didn't seem to occur to him how extremely unlikely it was for that ever to happen, not to mention the inappropriate paternalistic aspect. Government providing protections does not feel inappropriate to me—it feels like what humane countries should do.

I chose not to say that, though, but repeated that I wasn't suggesting solutions—I was simply trying to set the agenda.

We pay a big price in America because we spend so much time

trying to put the other side down, and so little time trying to work together.

The most surprising thing I realized after doing a show for five years is how unusual it is in television to put the needed focus on the people in real need in our country. I guess it's an occupational hazard for most longtime career journalists to maintain a certain detachment. Also, there is the incredible preoccupation with ratings, which translates into staying on the air. (I guarantee you that shows about hunger, the homeless, or prison reform are not ratings-getters.) Not being a longtime career journalist, I didn't have much detachment, and frankly, while I certainly didn't want to be canceled, I worried about it a lot less than most, at least as far as making a living was concerned. I clearly wasn't in it for the money, because in a relatively short time in the movies I could earn a year's cable-television salary. So circumstances allowed me to have this unique role of being a human rights advocate on television. However, that created something of a problem.

I had just aired the show of which I am most proud. I went to the Bedford Hills Correctional Facility in New York, a maximum security prison, and interviewed four women whose cases I had carefully studied as prime candidates for clemency. They had all been sentenced under the cruel Rockefeller Drug Laws. These laws call for a mandatory sentence of fifteen years to life if you are convicted of possession of four ounces of cocaine or sale of two ounces. One of these women was an addict. One was enticed by a "friend" into selling, so that the "friend" could reduce his sentence and pick up some cash from the police. Another was asked to get some cocaine by her cousin who was asked by a "friend" who was a police informant. An appeals court judge said there was no proof that another woman was selling or using but only dating a drug dealer. All were young mothers. None had prior records. All could have served lesser sentences if they had taken a plea bargain, but they had chosen to go to trial. Two got mandatory sentences of twenty years to life and the other two, fifteen to life. They have served a combined total of about fifty years. One's children have been put in foster care. Another's former husband denies her existence to their daughter. Another's son took to the streets and is in prison. The law has been a disaster. They were all desperate, poor people. None of these people was a drug dealer. On the show I was joined by two nuns who worked on Rikers Island. I asked the nuns if they knew of any wealthy inmates. They said they knew of no wealthy or middle-class inmates, only poor ones. I felt it was the most compelling show I ever did.

The next day, I got a call from an NBC executive. He said to me, "You stumbled last night." Predictably, the show had gotten a lower rating than my norm. We're talking one-tenth of a ratings point here, minuscule numbers. He was very pleasant about it, though, and so was I when I asked if he had seen the show. He hadn't. I said I thought it was the most significant show I've ever done, and I'd send it to him. He didn't ask me not to do it again, but suggested I do that type of thing in the latter part of the show, after I "hook" the audience with impeachment talk or something. As I said, it was all very cordial, but it screamed out to me, *Content is irrelevant!* This was a business no different from a store that sells lamps. That strong awareness has never left me. I once asked a colleague who had his own show if he felt any obligation to do shows on social issues. He looked at me, smiled, and said, "If anyone will watch." I pressed ahead, trying to continue to focus on these problems and yet stay on the air, and I did. In five years of putting a focus on these subjects, along with the topical issues, I had one of the highest-rated shows on CNBC and MSNBC, and when it wasn't, it was in time slots where no one ever had been, before or since.

At this writing, there are over 2 million people in prison in America. There are only 8 million people in prison in the whole world. There are more people in prison in America than in any other country in the world. The number is up 70 percent in the last ten years! We represent 25 percent of the world's prison population and 5 percent of the world's overall population! Two-thirds of the people in prison are nonviolent—that's about 1.4 million nonviolent people in prison for long, long periods. We lock up thousands of mentally ill people who should be in hospitals instead. We spend more money on prisons than universities—$40 billion a year. And yet Madeleine Albright, when she was secretary of state, said we lacked the funding to properly secure the State Department from adversaries' surveillance. Prisons are great for local business.

Advocates for the present system argue that crime is down. There are many reasons for that. More police on the streets is a major one. I guess if we locked up 10 million people, we'd have no crime at all. The Supreme Court recently ruled that it was okay for a police officer to lock up a woman because she didn't have her and her kids' seat belts on!

A country where people are stopped walking down the street for no real reason will yield some law-breaking, but that's not America. Those are the kind of countries we go to war with.

I'm all for locking up people who deserve it. I'm asking that we take a harder look at exactly who's in prison, and why, and who isn't!

The Beginning of Trouble:
Andy Friendly Leaves

Somewhere in the middle of all of this, Andy Friendly, who brought me to CNBC, left CNBC. He took a job working for Michael and Roger King—King World—the people I was involved with when he came to get me. So I left King World to go to CNBC, and Andy left CNBC to go to King World.

Andy and I had a very warm relationship. I remember one day he was joined behind the camera by Suzanne Wright, the wife of Bob Wright, then president of NBC. It turned out that Suzanne and Bob were two of my biggest supporters, and that would make for some very interesting situations down the line when they encountered others in management who weren't.

When Andy left, I should have seen that was not a good omen for me, but my show had been nominated as best show in the talk show series category every year I'd been on the air, and I never felt I was in jeopardy. I was sorry to see Andy go, but I never viewed his leaving as a threat to me. I should have.

Mark Rosenweig was Andy's second in command, and he took Andy's job. I got along well with Mark. He was always saying,

"Never look at ratings on a nightly basis, look after six months." It was a relaxing sentiment, but I don't think it was ever true. I don't even know if Mark believed it. I think he was just being nice. Still, I wasn't looking over my shoulder, yet.

Now, I'm the kind of guy, weird as this may seem (but what's a memoir without the truth), who once walked down a hall, saw someone from management heading in my direction at the other end of the hall (in this case, Roger Ailes), and went up a staircase before he spotted me. I never had a bad moment with Roger, who, with Andy Friendly gone, was the one man left responsible for bringing me into television, and yet I knew Roger to be the type who shoots from the hip and doesn't worry too much about the consequences. He'd never done it directly to me, but I knew he'd attacked me to others, because one executive actually called me and said, "You can't believe what Roger said about you this morning." I quickly jumped in with "Whoa! I don't want to hear it." He once read a letter from a viewer to some others in management that criticized me in ways I can't even think of, so without Andy between us, who knew what Roger might say to me. In fairness to Roger, what top executive doesn't from time to time privately attack his talent?

Speaking of shooting from the hip, there was an NBC executive, Ed Scanlon, with whom I later became friends, but on first meeting me at a party he said, "Boy, those monologues do go on, don't they?" I just smiled at him. If I had answered him, I would have said, That's right, sometimes they do, and sometimes they're this and sometimes they're that, but they're always from the heart, and when you speak from there without a script, anything might happen, and the anything-might-happen part is more important than the other considerations. But I didn't say any of that. I just smiled. The proof of the pudding, in my opinion, was always in the ratings.

Ed Scanlon was a real character in the power hierarchy at NBC. He was the figure behind the scenes who took care of things most people didn't even know about. He was the consigliere, feared and loved, and he was going to play a significant role in my life on cable.

Back to Roger Ailes. Once I got a call from Mark Rosenweig, who told me Roger wanted me to know that on the previous night Geraldo had gotten a very high rating (with a show on O. J. Simpson). I had gotten a very low rating with my lead guest, a not extraordinarily well-known celebrity, and following me, Bob Berkowitz had gotten a very high rating with his show, *Real Personal,* which again, more graphically than you'd imagine, discussed sex. I said to Mark I was aware of all of that, and what did Roger want me to do with that information? Mark said, "Roger just wanted you to know." I took that as a warning shot, so I said, "Tell Roger if I did shows on O. J. Simpson or sex, I could get high ratings as well." Then, necessity being the mother of invention, I began to do shows on O. J. Simpson and guess what—we got very high ratings, sometimes the highest on the network. Once we began to do the Simpson shows, all was quiet from headquarters. I think I may have even dared pass Roger in the hall once and exchanged a high five.

Then it seemed that in no time at all Roger was gone as well—not only Roger but the whole other network he started, America's Talking (sister network to CNBC)—and MSNBC was born. I'm sure there are many versions of what actually happened here, of why Roger wasn't running MSNBC. He told me it would have meant reporting to Andy Lack, who was the head of NBC News, and Roger wasn't all that big in the "reporting to" department. I mean, he ran the media end of the senior George Bush's campaign for the presidency, and he's had enormous success in television, and Roger wasn't going to report to Andy Lack, and that was that. So Roger left, and around the same time so did Mark Rosenweig, also to go to King World, which meant all the executives responsible for bringing me to CNBC were gone. It's a given in the movie industry that if there's a change at the top of a studio where you have a movie that's been given a green light, or is already in production or about to come out, it's never good news. The same could be said of what was happening at CNBC. I was perceived as Roger Ailes's guy or Andy Friendly's guy. That's not to say that others such as Geraldo or Chris Matthews didn't overcome that fact, but most didn't.

In came two men named Bill Bolster and Bruno Cohen. Bill is a big blustery man who looks like he might have been a cheerleader at an earlier time. Bruno looks like an introverted professor who has a lot of secrets. Bill and Bruno had enormous success running the local New York City NBC station, WNBC, and now they were in charge of CNBC.

Bill invited me to join him and Bruno for dinner shortly after they took over. Within a minute of sitting down, Bill told me there were people who felt he should run for governor of Iowa. I looked at him for a moment and told him there were people who felt I should run for governor of Connecticut. Dinner was a lot of fun. Bruno sat there and observed, as Bill and I made each other laugh for the next two hours. At a second dinner, with just Bill and me (this time, at my request, he drove to Connecticut), we again had a lot of fun. At that meeting, Bill made certain proclamations about how large an audience CNBC, under his aegis, would eventually have. I stared at him and said, "As a friend, I advise you not to say this stuff publicly." It was good advice. As has been proven over and over again, there is a limit to how many people are interested in endless hours of discussion on political and legal issues, but Bill wasn't all that interested in hearing about limits. It's actually not a bad trait for a president of a company, as long as he keeps his totally unrealistic projections in the locker room, so to speak.

Shortly after he arrived on the scene, Bill marched over to my executive producer, Marlene Dann, and asked, "What type of show do you do that gets the highest rating?" Without missing a beat, she said, "O. J. Simpson shows." He said, "You don't have to look it up?" "No," she said. He quickly said, "Well, I want you to get just as high ratings with your other shows as you do with the Simpson shows." Marlene just stared at him, as he marched away. The next day, Bill phoned Marlene to inquire what show we did the preceding night that got a huge rating. "O. J. Simpson," Marlene said easily.

Marlene had a most appreciated ability to make things run smoothly for me. Part of this had to do with her putting together a staff that included Alice Hurwit and Anne Hilbert, two of the kindest, most professional people I've ever met. It's not an easy feat to *always* hold it together, particularly when you're doing live one-hour shows.

Of course, it's important to understand boundaries in all relationships, and these three women excelled at this little-talked-about but crucial element in professional relationships.

When I was working in the movies, I would always have a talk with the director early on and tell him that in the course of filming I might have a number of ideas.

What I wanted from the director was that he or she listen to them. The next part of the conversation was key. I said that whether you liked what I had to say or not, I would act the same way. In other words, if you disagreed with me, I wouldn't act any different than if you agreed. There'd never be any "attitude" from me.

Also, once the people in charge understood what I was saying, whether they responded or not, I'd get off the subject, so I wouldn't wear them down. Respecting the chain of command, for me, is essential. You can have all the ideas in the world, but you also have to have a sense of humility that allows you to know you just might be wrong.

Marlene Dann, Alice Hurwit, and Anne Hilbert seemed to know all of this, so they made working with them a great pleasure.

Bruno Cohen, Bill Bolster's number two, was the opposite of Bill in personality. As with Bill, I liked Bruno. In fact, I liked Bruno a lot. Bruno always looked like he was telling you about 10 percent of what he knew. I'm sure that's true of a lot of people in management, but with Bruno it was blatant. Sometimes he looked as though he actually had to bite his tongue from spilling the beans on the 90 percent he was holding back.

Early on he told me of a sales meeting where one of the salespeople wanted to know if "Grodin was going to keep doing those monologues." The salesperson said they could be controversial, implying that maybe that wasn't good for business. Bruno told me he told the sales force that the monologues were "incredibly generous of Grodin, that it costs him a lot to reach down deep and say all that." I never thought of it that way, but who was I to contradict the head of programming?

As for being controversial and scaring advertisers, another executive at the top of NBC told me that the advertisers in fact "love

With the staff from my CNBC show. From left to right: Anne Hilbert, John Gabriel, executive pro-
ducer Marlene Dann, me, Alice Hurwit, Kathy Fiume, and Clay Dettmer. The show was about the
best experience I've ever had—until management changed.

you, because your rating doesn't go down in the course of the hour, even though, as it gets later, there are fewer viewers available."

It didn't take long for me to be personally affected by the change at the top. I had for some time changed the structure of my show so that when the guest was a celebrity, I would delay the celebrity's appearance to best sustain the rating throughout the hour. I would do the monologue and then some special type of humor for the major part of the first half hour, then bring on the celebrity. It's the same structure for *The Tonight Show* and David Letterman.

I was out in Los Angeles with my mother, who was in the hospital with an illness that ultimately took her life. At the time, we didn't know that was going to happen. I was using substitute hosts for about a week, and then because things seemed to be stable at the hospital, I said I'd go to the Los Angeles studio, as we had an opportunity to have Jerry Seinfeld return as a guest. Jerry was clearly a supporter of the show. He even did a *Seinfeld* episode where he was scheduled to appear on my show and was nervous about what he would talk about. He had a bottle of hot sauce or something with a picture of a guy who looked like me, and it was accidentally broken. The episode showed Jerry pacing in what was supposed to be my green room, and on the wall was a full-length portrait of me. It reminded me of the time I went to visit this couple who were friends of mine in Los Angeles, and the woman had a full-length portrait of herself in a gown above the fireplace. I laughed when I saw it. Since the woman works in comedy, I assumed it was a joke. I quickly was told it wasn't. It still struck me as funny.

Anyway, consistent with the structure of my show, Jerry Seinfeld came out after my friend Richard Martini, who told a funny story. I saw Richard as kind of an opening act. Shortly after that, I read in the papers, of all places, about Bill Bolster's feeling about the whole thing. It was something about how I kept Seinfeld waiting so that I could have a college buddy on (Richard Martini I think is at least twenty years younger than I am, so it was kind of an inadvertent compliment, and no, in case you're wondering, I've never had any "work" done). Bill then went on to express his displeasure that when I did get Jerry out there, I did most of the talking. Clearly, that was Bill's impression, and just as clearly in his position, you don't say that for media consumption. I wrote him a note letting him know it wouldn't be awkward if we ran into each other in the halls, and as a joke I threw in, "It obviously won't impact on our skinny-dipping sessions in the Y pool." I think he liked that joke, because he would often refer to it when he saw me. Bill always preferred jokes to talking about what I was doing on the network.

Once I think he was ordered by the powers above him, meaning Ed Scanlon, to bring me a cake after my five hundredth show. As he presented the cake, he said, "If I was in those movies with you, they would have grossed even more." I responded, "I wish you were in the movies, because I'd give anything to get you out of this building." There was a lot of nervous laughter on that one.

On another occasion, I was quoted in the papers as saying something not about Bill, but that Bill didn't like (I honestly can't even remember what it was), but I went to see him about it, and he threw one of his shoes at me (and he has a big foot, too). It reminds me of the people who worked for Ronald Reagan talking about him throwing things at them and saying that if he was really mad he didn't throw anything. Anyway, Bill threw his shoe, it missed, I sat down, and we again had some good laughs for about twenty minutes. Humor does conquer all, at least temporarily.

It wasn't that funny, though, on the day when my producer and close friend Clay Dettmer was driving me to work and said something like Howard Stern is on the radio saying you're going to be canceled. At the time, Clay, who had need-to-know instructions about what and what not to tell me, felt correctly that I needed to know that, because it could very well be true. Unfortunately I was already flat on my back in the car from a lower-back condition that had flared up, I'm sure from some other less-than-good news. The reason I believed what Stern had said was that earlier there had been an in-house presentation of the coming season's shows, and we weren't mentioned. When my producer asked about it, they said, "We forgot."

Clay, who worked with me for ten years, is a very bright Yale graduate with a uniquely positive disposition. Once at the end of a day I said to him, "Well, that was a good day." He gave me one of his ear-to-ear grins and said, "They're *all* good days, Chuck." At that moment, with that Stern report of my imminent cancellation, even Clay would have been hard-pressed to call this a good day.

I immediately called Jim Griffin at William Morris, who called Ed Scanlon, who called Bill Bolster, who was instructed to call me to let me know I wasn't going to be canceled. In fact Bill was instructed to tell me I was going to be renewed. Then Bill said in a very uncharacteristic, almost plaintive tone, "You didn't have to go outside the building. I was going to renew you." I said in a very matter-of-fact tone, "That's not the impression I got." So by the evening, Clay was right. It *was* a good day.

The next change at the network was really mind-boggling. I don't believe it was done directly as a move on me, but that was the result. Reruns of Conan O'Brien were going to be put on in my time slot at ten, where I had, then and now, gotten the highest ratings in the network's history, and I would be moved to eleven.

I thought it was a terrible idea. Conan O'Brien is a topical late-night comedy show. Having a rerun of him following *Rivera Live,* which dealt mostly with big court cases, would give virtually no audience flow. It was just the wrong place, the wrong time, and, by any standard, a bad idea. He would not get the Geraldo audience, and what audience he did get surely wouldn't stay tuned for another issues show, which by that time was what we had largely become. Also, Conan was mostly a celebrity-interview show, and we had learned that our occasional celebrity interviews were among the lowest rated of our shows.

Conan, by the way, had been a hilarious guest on my show when he described the critical onslaught when he was set to replace David Letterman at NBC. Conan invented the character Chip Wheatly as his alter ego and answered a question about his qualifications by saying, "I graduated college."

Conan following Geraldo was even worse than I thought. It was as strange as putting Ted Koppel and *Nightline* on Comedy Central. By the time the Conan rerun ended, there often was no discernible rating at all. Hash marks are what they're called. Conan was out there in his opening talking about Bob Dole's chances in the election—a month after the election. Conan has become a real success in late night and, of course, it was a disservice to him to expose him after Geraldo, in reruns yet.

Just prior to Conan's coming on, management made a really bizarre request. They wanted my staff and me to view these Conan reruns and try to incorporate material from them into my monologues.

One of the executives actually said, "It's a great opportunity, be-cause you get to see them ahead of time, and it will make it more like Conan and you are part of the same network."

Very few things leave me speechless, but that request did.

I placed my one and only call to Don Ohlmeyer at NBC, who held a position above the executives who made the request. With-out mentioning who gave me the note, I asked his opinion of the request.

Without even the slightest hesitation he said, "Just keep doing what you're doing. Keep taking your best shot with that high hard one." Don, of course, has an extensive sports background.

I was comfortable calling Don because earlier he had sent me a warm note in which he referred to me as "one of the cornerstones of the network."

The note from Don was motivated by my having talked about him on the air during the O. J. Simpson trial. I had made the point that nobody was more unrelentingly critical of Simpson than I was, and one of my bosses, Don Ohlmeyer, was among Simpson's clos-est friends, and I had never been asked by him or anyone working for him to tone it down.

Later Don had some exchanges with members of the media over their coverage, but never with me.

A note that topped the "incorporate Conan's show into your show" note was one about my mother.

From the time I came on the air, I always ended my show by say-ing, "Good night, Mom, I love you." After my mother passed, I chose to continue to say it.

One executive said to me, "I'd like to see something at the end of the show in addition to the fact that you still love your mother."

There really was nothing wrong with that note, except I can think of a couple of better ways to say it.

Prior to Conan's debut, Bruno Cohen sat with me in my office and told me that he had to put in writing for Bob Wright and the other people in charge what his projection was for the Conan-rerun rating. I think it was a .8 in the fall when all this took place, and a 1.5 come spring. With a full-page ad in *USA Today* and tremendous promotion, it debuted with a .7. I took yet a little higher .7 at eleven o'clock, not a good sign, and very soon with enough Bob Dole jokes, weeks after the election, it understandably plunged. Bruno had also said to me that if this didn't work out the way he projected, he would soon be gone. That didn't seem quite fair, since all of management seemed to be behind the idea of Conan.

One executive referred to it as "a win–win idea." I never asked what that meant, but I always felt like it was more of a lose–lose idea.

It wasn't too long before Bruno was gone. Happily, he wasn't asked to leave the building, but instead was put in charge of daytime, which was all stock-market reports and programs. This move coincided with the upward move of the market, so Bruno thrived.

Bill Bolster remained in charge and in came a reluctant Bridget Potter to take Bruno's position as head of programming. I say reluctant because Bridget was already in charge of NBC late night, which included Conan's show, and also still had responsibilities from a previous job at HBO.

I had known Bridget for twenty-five years. Even when she wasn't, she always appeared to be in charge of something. She came in full of good cheer, proclaiming, "Bob Wright wants you in the NBC family, as long as you want to be on television."

Bridget brought with her an amiable fellow named Bob Reichblum, who sometimes rocked on the balls of his feet as he talked. In the past Bob had worked for *Good Morning America*, among other shows. As Bill Bolster and Bruno Cohen had done, Bridget and Bob Reichblum suggested we have dinner, and I agreed. Everyone was very friendly, and it was enjoyable, until we got out into the parking lot and Bob, cheerful as always, asked how he should get in touch with me. I just as cheerfully said, "Regarding what?" Bob, topping my pleasantness, said, "Thoughts on the show." Now you may ask, what's wrong with that? Well, it's a good question. If you want to say, as Andy Friendly did earlier, "How about not having a singer every night?" that's fine. If you want to say, as Bruno Cohen did, "How about just coming up cold without the opening titles?" fine. However, as I've said, the possibility always exists that someone's going to come along and say, "I thought you talked too much," or, "You let the guest talk too much." It's called micromanaging, and it makes for uptight, self-conscious hosts. I've seen that over and over. (Some hosts agree to let the control room talk to them during the show by wearing a device in their ear. Not for me!) As I've said, while you must be able to take criticism, you must understand that for every good note, there can be ten bad ones, and they will ruin you. So you want to be careful and protected if you can. I said, "Just talk to Marlene Dann [my executive producer] whenever you want, and I'm sure she'll bring me whatever's appropriate." When he looked a little taken aback, standing there between cars in the parking lot, I quickly said I could really get self-conscious with performance notes. He just as quickly said he understood. Bob and Bridget drove away in their car and I in mine, with all of us I'm sure wondering what was coming next.

It quickly revealed itself. Bob Reichblum, who's a hardworking and dedicated fella, began to call daily meetings with the staffs of all the shows to go over what everyone was doing. There could have been a real benefit to this regarding repetition of guests. For example, if we had an outstanding guest for our O.J. show at eleven who had been booked for a week, it probably wasn't a good idea for Geraldo's excellent aggressive producers to book that guest on the same day to be on before us. That's exactly what happened, and since Geraldo's show was almost always the highest-rated show on the network, especially with us following the Conan rerun, no one wanted to tell his producers not to do it.

The daily meetings with my staff went on and on. I kept waiting for someone to tell me some good idea that came out of them, but I never heard one. Mostly what I heard was a lot of micromanaging about this and that, most of which my staff spared me. Somewhere in there, Janice Lieberman's fine show, *Steals and Deals,* where she uncovered consumer fraud, was canceled, after her staff was thoroughly demoralized, the same way my staff was becoming. Keep in mind, the goal of all of this was to increase ratings. The best idea would have been to drop the Conan rerun, restore me to 10 P.M., and continue with Rivera and Grodin back to back, but that didn't happen. Month after month went by, as the audience deserted CNBC after Geraldo when the Conan rerun came on. Everyone knew this wouldn't last, but I guess an early cancellation would have been embarrassing to people who just weren't going to be embarrassed.

Some of the notes from up top did, by obligation, get through to me, and here once again I'm not going to mention names. Let's just say they came from management. I want to illustrate them, not to hurt anyone but to specifically point out how destructive and too often useless and demoralizing such notes can be.

In one of the many shows we did on race relations, we opened the show, which was taped, with a clip of Martin Luther King, Jr., saying a man should be judged by the content of his character and not the color of his skin. After the taping, Marlene Dann told me there was a request from management that we change the opening and not use the clip. I asked why, and Marlene, of course, fully understanding how absurd it was, said, "They feel it's not young and current." In other words, it would have been preferable to begin the show with a racist event that happened that day, preferably between young people, to attract the desirable 18–49 or 25–54 audience they were always after. Since we didn't have a current racist event, we stayed with Martin Luther King. I shudder even now as I write this.

The emphasis on the 18–49 or 25–54 grew and grew over the years to the point that any talk of "ratings" was considered not only irrelevant but an annoyance. The younger group used to be called "demos" and then were simply called "adults," suggesting to me anyway that if you were over fifty-four, you might still be an adult, but not the kind the executives had any interest in. The theory is that after fifty-four, people are set in their ways, and you'll never persuade them to buy anything other than what they already buy. It is acknowledged that people over fifty-four may actually have the highest buying power, but it's thought they're just not changeable. Now a new theory is emerging that just possibly the older audience is a lot more important than originally perceived. It all feels like Woody Allen's movie *Sleeper*, set in the future, when it's discovered that fat is good for you.

Another stunning note came after a show we did on bullies. I always felt that at the heart of just about every school shooting was bullying. The killers, almost always, were first verbally and sometimes physically abused by their classmates. With all due respect to the horrific influence of violence in the movies, television, and video games, it seems to me most of the time these shootings wouldn't have happened without first making the killers feel powerless to deal with the crushing abuse they endured. Of course, that doesn't mean that every kid who is bullied will kill—just some of them.

On our bullies show, we had some video of a boy in a schoolyard being pushed, shoved, and then knocked down and kicked over and over. The assault lasted about a minute and fifteen seconds. Of course, the seemingly unending nature of it, similar to the Rodney King beating, is what made it particularly horrifying. After the show, I heard that the feeling was we let the clip run too long, that the point could have been made in much less time. Of course, a large part of the point was how long it went on. That's why at the Rodney King trial there wasn't an abbreviated version to spare the viewers. I figure if the kid is beaten and kicked that long, we can at least watch it. Obviously the image starts to burn into your brain more and more the longer it goes on. Imagine, God forbid, it was your kid. The criticism that we let the clip run too long totally missed the point.

There was a great deal of disbelief from management when I refused to have Howard Stern on. It's not that I had to have the highest respect for every guest we booked, but this guy, to quote my friend the playwright Herb Gardner, represented "the last stop be-fore the end of civilization."

Everyone needs a reality check from time to time, and Herb Gardner has served as one for me and countless others for years. He's extraordinarily bright, and while his sense of right and wrong in the professional world may seem lofty and unrealistic to some, he is an outstanding moral barometer to a lot of us who try to nav-igate the minefields of the arts and media.

Then there was David Letterman. I'd been appearing with David for several years, so when we asked him to do an hour with me, he readily agreed, even though he seldom appears. Anyway, just as with Jerry Seinfeld, it was a real coup for CNBC to have David Letter-man appear on their network. David preferred to do the interview from his office, which was not a problem for me, as many of our guests appeared on the satellite with me in the studio. Suddenly, there were expressions of disbelief that I wasn't going to Letter-man's office for the interview. I had never gone anywhere to inter-view anyone. We always did the show from the CNBC studios in Fort Lee with me on my set. The idea of going to someone's office or hotel room never occurred to me. If I had gone to David Letter-man's office, the next time a major name was booked and wanted me to come to his or her office or hotel room, what's my explanation for not doing it? Letterman's a bigger name? So going to David's office seemed a bad idea any way you looked at it. I was perceived as diffi-cult for holding my position. I heard very little "It's great you got Letterman." The rating, of course, went way up for the show, but all I heard was, "It would have been even higher if Chuck had gone to Dave's office." A couple of months later, I had a chat with an NBC executive and told him the story. He said, "We wouldn't want you to go to Letterman's office!" Clearly, there had been some bad feeling between some at the top of NBC and David Letterman at his being passed over for the host position on *The Tonight Show*. David had been unrelenting in his digs at NBC before and after the decision was made, and years later there were still negative feelings on all sides.

For my five hundredth show, I was able to get my friend Jack Paar to join me along with Regis Philbin. Prior to my show, Regis had rarely, if ever, appeared on CNBC, and Jack never there and hardly anywhere. I met Jack Paar several years ago at a gathering at Regis and Joy Philbin's house.

Jack and I became friends immediately and began to go out to dinner regularly. Once a small group of us were in a restaurant that had a fellow playing the piano. It was a little difficult to hear the conversation, so I went to the manager, who was standing nearby

I said, "I'm sitting over there with Jack Paar, and the music is making it a little difficult to hear the conversation." The manager's jaw dropped. He said, "You're sitting over there with who?" I said, "Jack Paar." Without a moment's hesitation, the manager looked over at the piano player and made a slashing motion across his neck, signaling for him to stop the music, which he instantly did.

Even though he's chosen to be out of the public eye for many years, the impact Jack made on our culture remains powerful for many of us.

They don't call them legends for nothing.

The five hundredth show was wonderful, with Jack and Regis hilarious, along with outstanding clips from the first four hundred ninety-nine shows. We had about ten people off camera to give a little feedback, chuckles, laughs, etc. All I heard afterward was that someone in management said, "I don't think the audience worked." When I repeated this observation to some people who had seen the show, they all said the same thing: "What audience?" This audience was such a tiny element in this hour, most people wouldn't have thought even to mention it.

Again, I cite all this to show that not all notes are constructive, even though the people giving them are well intentioned.

People have said to me, "Didn't you get a lot of notes in the movies?" In my case, the answer is no. By the time most people are hired for Broadway or the movies, you can bet they've been chosen over hundreds of others and paid a lot of money. The best you can do as a director or producer is create an environment in which performers can be at their best. Again, none of this is to say that there aren't such things as excellent notes. I also want to be clear that I never express annoyance or irritation if someone chooses to give me bad notes. I know they mean well, and I focus on the fact that they consider it their responsibility and are trying to contribute. I just want to again point out here that "constructive criticism" is more rare than people think, and often the critics are just dead wrong.

A good example of this is a movie I did years ago called *11 Harrowhouse*. When it was screened prior to opening, it got about 50 percent excellent, very good, or good on the preview cards. That's terrible. It means the picture will be a failure. I got the idea along with my friends Herb Gardner and Elaine May to put in a narration throughout the picture. It was kind of a comedic voiceover. After I did this and the picture was screened again, the excellent, very good, and good added up to 92 percent, which is extremely high. It doesn't mean it's a hit. It just means it has a much better

Someone once said that the way to remain a legend is never to appear. That didn't stop the legendary Jack Paar from joining legend-in-the-making Regis Philbin and me on my five hundredth show on CNBC.

chance. When the critic from *Variety* reviewed it, he said I had "almost ruined" the picture with the narration. The picture wasn't a hit, but the studio heads felt the box-office gross was tremendously increased by the narration.

As the new management continued to assert itself at CNBC, things got worse.

First, there were some excellent regular guests who management felt shouldn't be booked anymore for various incredibly subjective reasons. The most offensive comment I ever heard in those five years of television came from an executive whose name I will again mercifully omit. This person literally shouted at my producer, "No more old people!" referring to two guests, both household names, who recently hadn't been that successful. To me, a person's stature is measured not by what he last did, but by a body of work, and by that standard, both guests were giants!

When I pointed out to the executive that one of these guests always delivered a high rating, there was an awkward silence. Then the executive said, "I'd like to see you one on one with ———— [a prominent TV newsman]." When I pointed out that I was a real fan of this person and had gone one on one with him more than once and it always got a low rating, there was more silence.

Also, there was passionate objection to another type of show I would sometimes do. These shows came under the heading of "coping with life." We would have the type of questions that might be raised in a Dear Abby column and hear what people on the street had to say. These issues that may seem like nothing, unless they're happening to you, are, in my experience, capable of taking over your daily life.

The question could be whether you should lend someone

money. I can quickly think of more than a couple of friendships that ended over money. The irony is, it wasn't because I didn't lend them money, but because I did. They were unable or unwilling to pay me back, so they dropped out of sight. Even after I told one fellow I didn't want the money back, he was too embarrassed to stay in touch.

One friend called to ask for two thousand dollars. I said, "Okay," and then he said, "How about twenty-five hundred?" I said, "Sure." Then he said, "How about three thousand?" I said, "What's happening here?" There wasn't a good answer. I sent him some money. I forget how much. I haven't seen or heard from him in twenty years.

One coping question plenty of people identify with might be: What do you do if you're at some kind of function and you run into someone to whom you're basically not even speaking? It could be someone whom you'd hoped never to see again—in this lifetime anyway.

A couple of years ago President Clinton found himself face-to-face with Fidel Castro at a UN function. There was no photograph, but it was reported they shook hands. *The New York Times* called it "acceptable diplomatic behavior."

A friend of mine who works in public relations says he has about five different levels of snubbing someone depending, of course, on their perceived offense. He also suffers from back problems.

Sometimes we would have a psychologist sitting with me, or I would go off camera to where the producers were sitting or the wife of a producer or a young woman just working in the building. It was fun, and you never knew from whom you would hear a valuable insight. The off-camera responses were ridiculed by management. It was seen to be Small, and this particular executive wanted Big. I was never sure exactly what Big meant other than a lot of graphics and music and horns and whistles. For me, Small meant more personal and better. My philosophy had been shared by Andy Friendly, whom I was missing more and more.

A really interesting development came when it was deemed a good idea to bring in a consultant for the show, a concept common in television. I told the executives and the consultant when I had lunch with him that it would be very difficult for anyone to come into a show that had been on the air for years and offer ideas that had not already been done or considered by the ten very smart people who were working there.

I liked this fellow, but to management's dismay, he quickly became less of a consultant and more of an advocate for the show. He too realized before long that new concepts were literally nowhere to be found. There was no type of show he suggested that we hadn't done, so he began to focus on getting us more promotion and got management to allocate three hundred dollars for me to get new ties, which I liked less than my old ties. Also, he made some kind of deal with a clothing manufacturer for me to get free suits, for a clothing credit. I didn't like the idea of endorsing a clothing line and ultimately decided against it. Soon he was off to another commitment in Europe, where he advised various media operations in different countries what a good idea it would be for them to buy shows like *Montel* or *Ricki Lake*. I liked the guy, but I gave my new ties away.

Jack Welch

Around this time, I thought it would be a good idea to make the acquaintance of Jack Welch, who ran General Electric, which owned, among other things, companies that manufacture a lot of the appliances we have in our houses, as well as NBC, CNBC, and MSNBC. When I first mentioned this idea to George Jamison, who had recently come to CNBC from his public relations duties at General Electric, he looked startled. I later learned that other than having pressing matters to discuss with him, not many people would seek a meeting with Jack Welch. I'd heard he was tough—in fact, his nickname was Neutron Jack, presumably because like the neutron bomb, he could eliminate thousands of people while buildings remained standing. Downsizing, they call it. Later, in the one meeting I had with Andy Lack, who now was in charge of NBC News, CNBC prime time, and all of MSNBC, he expressed aston ishment that I had actually gone to Jack Welch's office. "I've never been to his office," Andy explained. For me it was no big deal. In the movies, when I would go around promoting this picture or that, I always thought it was fitting to meet the guy who ran the studio, on the theory that if he was aware of what I was doing it might benefit me. Foolish optimism.

Once, many years ago, I was represented by the agency headed by the then so-called most powerful man in Hollywood, Mike Ovitz. When I went over to meet the agents, I asked to meet Mike. I was told I couldn't because Mike was too busy or too powerful, or something. I left that agency shortly thereafter. When I told that story to my friend Peter Falk, he stared at the floor Columbo-like for a very long time, then looked at me with wonderment and said, "They wouldn't let you meet the agent."

While I knew about the Neutron Jack thing, I didn't know at the time of another story I later read in a slim volume called *Jack Welch Speaks*. It told of one of the top G.E. executives passing Jack in the hall (this guy hadn't shot up a stairway), and Jack greeted him warmly with something like, "How ya doin'? Anything I can do for you?" The executive responded, "Yeah, you can stop calling me every lousy name in the book behind my back." To which Jack responded, "I'll call you any name I want!" So much for "Anything I can do for you?" So Jack was clearly not a guy to toy with, but since I was just going to meet him and not confront him, I wasn't worried. George Jamison, who accompanied me, was a little concerned though. Just to protect himself prior to the meeting, George casually said, "You're not planning to discuss your salary with Jack, are you?" I guess because most people had seen me with Johnny Carson and David Letterman, they might think I'd be capable of that.

In fairness, once I did go on Letterman's show and pointed out to him that although I'd been appearing with him for fifteen years, I was being paid the same as someone who was on for the first time, and since that was true, could he get me free tickets to Radio City

Music Hall? Of course, it was a joke, but the way it was presented, I'm sure plenty of people just thought I wanted those free Music Hall tickets.

Jack Welch's office, as I recall, had no door but a sliding wall. Once in, I immediately went into a boxing stance and sparred with him for a few moments. I have no idea why I did that. Maybe it's because Jack is trim and wiry and looks like a former lightweight boxer. Maybe it was a version of Bill Bolster saying to me there was talk of him running for governor of Iowa and my letting him know there was talk of me running for governor of Connecticut. That's guys for you!

When Jack and I stopped sparring, we sat down for about half an hour. He let me know he felt the network could do more with synergy (somehow promoting all its properties with one another). It was a nice feeling. He wanted to convey that he was thinking about ways to help us all. Then he said, "I'll get you on *The McLaughlin Group*." G.E. for years had sponsored John McLaughlin and his guest pundits across the country. I told him I had done an hour one on one with McLaughlin, and I'd send him some excerpts I thought he'd enjoy, which I did. I never was asked to join *The McLaughlin Group*, and I never got a response to the tape I sent. About a year later when I ran into Jack at an NBC gathering, I asked him if he'd seen the tape, and he said, "Yes." That was it. I'm sure he had other things on his mind.

One of them might have been the PCBs in the Hudson River. There had been a lot of press attention given to the polluting of the Hudson River by G.E. plants. This happened long before the reign of Jack Welch, but I'm sure it was a constant thorn in his side, as G.E. argued that dredging the river would cause more harm than good, stirring up all the pollutants at the bottom. One of the obvious major disadvantages to the public of conglomerates' owning the airwaves is it would be unlikely you'd see a lot of G.E. pollutant stories on NBC or negative Disney stories on ABC, which Disney owns. That's not to say that the networks wouldn't cover bad news about their owners, but would the coverage really be as extensive as it would be if the news weren't about the owners? Absolutely not.

Never giving any of this a moment's thought, we booked Robert Kennedy, Jr., on the show. He is a leading environmentalist and he blasted away at G.E. and the PCBs it was responsible for in the Hudson. Later Marvin Kitman, the columnist for *Newsday*, wrote a long piece about me and cited the appearance of Robert F. Kennedy, Jr., as "the longest attack on G.E. on a G.E. owned network ever." I didn't personally believe at that time, as Marvin did, that this program was the reason why, in the middle of my fourth year at CNBC, I was abruptly canceled.

Canceled

First, I should say that while it was a surprise and hurtful, I knew for me it was going to be a good thing. After three and a half years of doing four hours of television a week with unscripted monologues, it was getting to be more of a grind than I had in mind. I always enjoyed it, but particularly those live ten o'clock shows on the O. J. Simpson trial started to add up after a while. I was very grateful when the trial came to an end, and while the executives at all the cable networks obviously didn't appreciate the drop in ratings, for me it was a relief.

It certainly was an enjoyable job, and yet I was like football coaches who say they wouldn't mind a break. I had been talking with a couple of friends about preferring to go to two shows on the weekend, and that was my plan, to request that when the year came to an end.

One afternoon, I came up to my office after a taping, and one of my producers and excellent right-hand man Clay Dettmer said I should call Jim Griffin at William Morris, that it was important. By the look on Clay's face, I knew I hadn't won an award. Jim got on the phone immediately, saying that Andy Lack, the head of NBC News, wanted to terminate the show. The reason given was they could save NBC a lot of money by repeating *Hardball with Chris Matthews* at 11 P.M., rather than producing new programming at that hour, which no other cable network was doing except for live news or sports coverage. Chris had a show on at 8 P.M. that originally was called *Politics,* but at some point the name was changed to *Hardball,* a better title for Chris's style.

I was once at a gathering with Chris, who said to me, "If you come to Washington, I'll throw a party for you, and introduce you to a lot of people you won't like."

Since Andy Lack had been put in charge of prime time on CNBC and all of MSNBC, I had observed him looking me over on more than one occasion.

Once I was at a party at the house of the president of NBC, Bob Wright. It was a party Bob and his wife, Suzanne, gave in honor of their daughter and her husband, who were recently married. Their house is on a beautiful spot on the water in Connecticut.

A lot of the NBC, CNBC, and MSNBC brass and talent were there checking one another out. I remember Andy Lack staring at me across the lawn. Earlier at another gathering at NBC I remember Andy Lack staring at me across the room. I might just be imagining this, but it felt kind of like the stare a cat would give a mouse, or a spider a fly. I always tried to be talking to somebody important when Andy stared at me. I wanted him to feel I was friendly with people in high places. I was, too. I was very friendly with Bob and Suzanne Wright. I once called Bob's office and left a message asking if he and Suzanne would like to have dinner with my wife and me. I was pretty sure he'd accept for one reason: Suzanne was about my biggest fan.

Earlier Bob's office had called to see if my wife and I could sit next to his wife and him at some huge NBC thing at the Waldorf. When people who might want to get rid of you see you sitting with the president of the company, it's helpful.

Anyway, each time I've been with Bob and Suzanne, shortly thereafter I've been canceled. I know that sounds suspicious, but I'm telling you they're my biggest fans.

Bob once sent me an e-mail suggesting we run together for president and vice president after I made an on-air suggestion that Bob, instead of Donald Trump, run for president. I said, "At least no one calls him 'the Bob.' "

Marvin Kitman, for the long piece he wrote after my show's cancellation, used the headline TALK IS CHEAP, BUT RERUNS ARE CHEAPER STILL, CHUCK.

I mostly believe the real reason there was no one saying, let's protect the Rivera/Grodin combo at nine and ten, or let's worry about Grodin at eleven following the Conan rerun, or let's not take away his rerun at 1 A.M., was simple. It seemed to me that Andy Lack, the man now in charge of all this, preferred I not have a show in the first place. I'll give you some examples of why I say that, but I want to be clear: Just as with managers or coaches of sports teams, the people in these jobs have earned the right to exercise their judgment, so I never, then or now, had any bad feeling for Andy Lack. I completely disagree with him, but he's obviously entitled to his position.

When I first came to CNBC, hired by Roger Ailes, a longtime

rival of Andy's, Andy Lack wasn't running the cable networks; he was the head of NBC News. Jim Griffin made a suggestion to him about me one day in a rare phone call (Andy deliberately made himself fairly inaccessible). I had been doing my show for about six months, gotten great reviews, and soon would be nominated for my first Cable Ace Award when Jim suggested to Andy that maybe I should do some commentary for NBC, at the end of *Dateline* for example. Jim said Andy's response was, "Why would I do that? If I wanted to do that, I'd get Steve Martin. Bill Moyers does commentary." To many people, forgive me, I appeared to be a well-informed guy who asked interesting questions and spoke from the heart. To others—and clearly Andy was in this group—I was a guy who, about what seemed like ten minutes ago, was telling a Saint Bernard to get off a bed in a *Beethoven* movie. To Andy Lack, who had spent so many years in news, that must have seemed astonishing.

When Andy said why not get Steve Martin, it was clearly his way of saying Charles Grodin is a comedy actor and Steve Martin is a bigger one, so why not get Steve? In other words, there was no acknowledgment whatsoever that this guy Grodin was actually seen by some as a serious commentator. Andy as much as said it to me in the only meeting I ever had with him. If Andy Friendly could be described as a friendly bear, Andy Lack looks like the kind of bear who might try to do you in. He told me, seated with his associate David Corvo, and Jim Griffin, that his close friend Don Henley, the composer and singer from the Eagles, whom he and I greatly admired, watched me every night, and when he couldn't watch me, he taped me! He then said that Don had just called him the other night and said, "Did you hear what Grodin just said? Are you watching him?" Then Andy, in a bizarre moment in management/talent relations, told us that his response had been "Of course not." He actually said that with me sitting there. He said it fast. He said it low, but that's what he said. The meeting continued right on with everybody acting as though it was business as usual, as people often do when weird stuff happens.

In the arts, where I've spent most of my professional life, we don't have that elitism. We understand that someone can come seemingly from out of nowhere and do good work.

I believe one of the reasons Andy and others had a problem with my making the transition to a commentator's position so quickly was that, because of the fame that goes along with being an actor, they were not aware that for a very long time I had also been a writer.

The same thing is true of other actors. Most people don't know, for example, that Robert Shaw, the actor in *Jaws*, was an equally accomplished writer.

Later, when Jack Welch came down hard on the leaders of NBC to cut hundreds of millions in costs, it wasn't that difficult for Andy Lack to go to my supporters, Bob Wright and Ed Scanlon, and say, "We can save about three million dollars a year if we don't produce Grodin, who's only on at eleven, and give Chris Matthews a rerun." I was told Bob Wright's reaction to the financial inevitability of the decision was, "Oh, shit!"

I believe all this manipulation to move me out came from a fundamental belief held by Andy Lack—that, in truth, the public is best served if we hear only from lifelong journalists, preferably those based in Washington. I believe the public is best served by also hearing from people outside of Washington and in professions other than journalism. Lifelong anything in communications is not necessarily an outstanding attribute. For example, if all critics of actors had my background of years of study, their observations would be too inside. My perceptions of the fine points of that field might be appropriate for an essay, but in the long run, here too the public would be best served by hearing from some people who had an outside perspective rather than an inside one.

Many years ago, I was part of a radio seminar with movie critics where I dared to say, "I respect my friends' feeling about a movie as much as the opinion of a professional critic." One critic on the panel took clear offense and went out of her way to attack me whenever possible over the years. It was really striking in a Broadway show I did in 1975, *Same Time, Next Year*. It was standing-room-only the entire run. It was a two-character play. I won a best actor award, and this critic was the only reviewer out of fifty to pan me. So much for lifelong professional credentials and objectivity.

In past years, I tried to institute an audience survey that would be distributed at previews of Broadway shows to counterbalance the power of the critics in New York. It was gaining support until one powerful production-company head said, "That would be reducing opinion to the lowest common denominator." He meant the audience.

Having described what I believe Andy Lack's journalistic position is, I saw something recently that made me wonder. It was Memorial Day, and at ten o'clock I put on CNBC to catch Brian Williams's newscast, as I hadn't seen the news all day. It was preempted by a nature documentary! Then I remembered an effort once to preempt Brian's newscast on MSNBC, where it gets its first run. Brian and others made a lot of noise, and it wasn't done. It got into the papers and seemed odd—an all-news network preempts the evening news? Obviously this was not an all-news network, and just as obviously the position sometimes seems to be we don't want *anyone* on the network talking about issues if we can make more money with a nature documentary.

For whatever the actual reason, Andy Lack's point of view prevailed, and I was canceled.

As time has gone by, I have given more consideration to Marvin Kitman's thesis that I was canceled because I'd had on Robert Kennedy, Jr., and he'd attacked General Electric. I wonder how many other programs I did that made the powers that be unhappy. When you're that high rated and you keep being diminished, and then removed, it does make you wonder.

I remember my producer John Gabriel coming into the office, and it was like a scene from a movie as I told him the news of the cancellation. John looked completely stunned and felt for the sofa behind him as he slowly sat, never taking his eyes off me, hoping that it was just some dark joke. We were scheduled to have a staff meeting, but I really wanted some time to think of what to say to everyone, so I just said I'd be in touch tomorrow and left CNBC for what I knew was the last time. In hindsight, I probably should have gone back and done a farewell show, but a reflexive response took over. Even though I had really had enough and knew something else would emerge, it was an abrupt kiss-off.

After I was canceled, I received a phone call from Ralph Nader expressing his outrage over the cancellation of a show that he saw as an open door for people to come to speak on behalf of those who are rarely spoken for on television. He told me he'd called Jack Welch to register his protest, but Jack had chosen not to return the call.

A friend of mine once told me I was invaluable to Jack Welch because he could stand in front of his critics who accused him of being high-handed and not really caring about people with desperate problems, and say, "Charles Grodin does a show for us." When I told that story to an NBC executive, he chuckled, as though it were a joke. Jack Welch not returning Ralph Nader's call seems to confirm the executive's reaction.

In a few days, I kept a long-standing dinner engagement with Ed Scanlon. Ed had been an executive for RCA who was heavily involved when G.E. bought the company, and after the negotiations, Jack Welch asked Ed to join him. When Bob Wright began to run NBC, Jack sent Ed over to help in any way he could. In other words, Ed was somewhere in the stratosphere of power with Jack Welch and Bob Wright. Andy Lack was under all of them, but the way these things work, Andy had control of his own domain, the same as Dick Ebersol has over sports and, at the time, Don Ohlmeyer had over entertainment. So Andy had the control, but Ed Scanlon was still Ed Scanlon. His title was VP of Talent Relations. In fact, he was all over anything that mattered. He had stepped in in the past when Howard Stern had gleefully reported, probably with some true inside information, that I was about to be canceled, but this time with Jack Welch urging cost cutting, Andy Lack had made the case that carried the day—we can save money if we don't produce Grodin. Ed had already heard about the cancellation from two close cousins of his, who he said had asked him, "What are we supposed to do with Charles Grodin off the air?" He was also aware of the literally thousands of letters, faxes, e-mails, etc., that poured in after I was suddenly no longer there. What had begun as a professional relationship with Ed Scanlon had developed into a friendship.

Any discomfort between Ed and me over the cancellation quickly faded, as I told him that already my whole body was feeling different now that I was out from under the burden of producing four hours of television a week. I was, however, still interested in doing something, so I said to Ed, "This cancellation was a financial issue, right?" "Of course," he quickly said. "There's nothing personal here, right?" "Absolutely not," Ed said. I didn't share my feelings about Andy Lack's journalistic bias with Ed, since it was just speculation, and it was easier to present what I was interested in if we kept it on the financial question. I then said to Ed, "You are obligated to pay me for the next six months. Some of the staff is being retained. Why not put me on the weekend? It's what I actually prefer." He instantly brightened and said, "We could have you back-to-back with Tim Russert. I think you and Tim would be very strong back-to-back. Let me get into it."

After we finished dinner, Ed and I walked to the front of the restaurant. As we passed the bar area, two men leaped off their stools and came over to me, saying, "How can you be off the air? What's going on? You're the best thing they have!" and on and on. One was John Calipari, who was then the coach of the NBA's New Jersey Nets; the other was a well-known businessman in New York whom Ed knew of and I didn't.

When we reached the street Ed said to me, "How long did you have those guys planted at the bar?" "A couple of hours," I joked. We had a good laugh and went our separate ways.

While waiting to hear from Ed Scanlon, I went over for a visit with Roger Ailes, who was now running the Fox News Channel. Roger, I'm sure, felt at that point he should be one of the people running NBC and not Fox, and there are plenty of people, me included, who find him one of the smartest guys around.

Roger and I went back and forth at each other over liberal versus conservative concepts, and I finally made a point that Roger took, because he later repeated it to me, and even referenced it in letters he's since written me. Again, it is simply this: I don't know what the best solutions are for the various problems in our country. I'm just troubled by how little of the time they are brought front and center to be addressed in some way—liberal or conservative.

Roger and I talked in the abstract about his feeling that if I were to come to Fox, he'd like me to mix in more comedy with the commentary, which I had no problem with. Then he also seemed to say he'd like some give and take in our relationship. It was a reasonable thing to ask, and I said, "Sure," not really certain what it meant, although it had to be he gives and I take. At the time, I was fairly confident that an opportunity would be forthcoming for the weekends on CNBC, so nothing further was said, but I always felt I could have a show wherever Roger was.

Actually I have mixed feelings about Fox. On one hand, Roger is a friend, and I truly wish him well. On the other hand, the "We report, you decide" slogan is tough for me to take. Fox is obviously the most highly opinionated network, which is fine, but when you're watching Bill O'Reilly and Sean Hannity aggressively giving their opinions, far more than any other hosts on television, it's as though they're playing games with you with the "We report, you decide," hoping you won't notice.

In all the years I was on cable, there was probably no one more opinionated than I was, but if I had a slogan it would have to be, "This is what I think, you decide." Granted it's not as sharp as "We report, you decide," but it's a heck of a lot more honest.

I can't really watch O'Reilly or Hannity, and I'll tell you why. O'Reilly's always going on about how fair he is. I caught part of a debate he had with James Carville, where he was asked if he had anything good to say about President Clinton. He had been unmercifully bashing Clinton for a long time. I thought to myself, That's an easy one for him. He'll throw Clinton a crumb to show how "fair" he is. But he didn't. He acknowledged that the former president was at times capable of displaying "an appealing personality," but that was it. After eight years of many accomplishments, all he could say was sometimes the guy had an appealing personality.

Bill Clinton is the most frustrating of politicians. Even though I believe Ken Starr and his prosecutors did the country a real disservice by trying to turn lying about a consensual sexual relationship into a "high crime," it was Bill Clinton who, as has been said many times, gave them the opportunity. It was Bill Clinton who made it possible for the government's energy to be so wasted for so long, and that's unforgivable, but to say that the only thing about the former president that's positive is he could sometimes have an appealing personality is as offensive to me as saying that John McCain is against breast-cancer research, which was said during the New York primary.

It was the Clinton administration that finally got unpaid medical leave of up to twelve weeks for workers to take care of serious medical problems for themselves or their families without losing their jobs. That sounds like a no-brainer, but it was never law until the Clinton administration fought for it. It was also the Clinton administration that fought hard, unsuccessfully, to have "unannounced" visits to nursing homes so that we could better deal with the rampant abuses there.

Those are just a couple of examples of a very long list of what the former president's administration achieved or tried to achieve for people really in dire straits.

The bully side of Mr. O'Reilly's personality regularly leaps off the screen. I once read a column by him in the *New York Post* where he wrote the following with apparent pride: "My grandfather, a New York City cop, told me once that he didn't bother arresting suspected dope dealers on his beat—he just applied his nightstick to a sensitive part of their anatomies." But what if they actually weren't drug dealers, just innocent people getting whacked in their privates? And if they were drug dealers, you're obviously supposed to arrest them, not hit them, but O'Reilly seems proud of his grandfather. If my grandfather ever told me anything like that I wouldn't be proud of him, I'd be ashamed of him, and I'd sure never see fit to quote him, unless, of course, I was a bully as well.

O'Reilly sometimes displays keen intelligence and does often articulate a point of view that many of us can identify with, but his trumpeting how fair he is—even though he often isn't—coupled with his ever-present arrogance has me looking elsewhere for my news. At this writing, there's a promo on Fox where O'Reilly comes on and says something like, "Who's looking out for us working people?"

I really don't mean to be picky, but can you earn millions of dollars and still say "us working people"? Obviously he works, but still...

There was a book years ago called *When Bad Things Happen to Good People.* Someone should write a book called *When Bright People Say Stupid Things.* Some of O'Reilly's musings would go well there. He claims the real problem with America isn't racism as much as it is classism. He likes to talk about all the different working-class jobs he held, and says, "The heart of America's somewhat unfair social setup is class, not race." He claims, "The question for this age in America is: What class are you?" It doesn't seem to occur to him that maybe he didn't always get what he wanted because of his own failings, which had nothing whatsoever to do with where he grew up or what schools he attended.

By O'Reilly's perception of life in America, the fact that I used to be a cabdriver and a night watchman, and I didn't go to an Ivy League school, really worked against me!

He proudly proclaims his "No Spin Zone," which I take to mean that in his presence only the truth is allowed. Of course, that's the truth according to O'Reilly. "No Spin" allows him to be rude, aggressive, and remarkably hostile. He obviously knows that hostility expressed provokes hostility right back at you. Many have tried it before him. It has paid off in the short run, but never the long.

Finally, the very title of O'Reilly's show, *The O'Reilly Factor,* represents his out-of-control ego. While many of us have had our names in the titles of our shows, for, I believe, legitimate identification purposes, to call yourself a factor would be like my calling my show *The Charles Grodin Influence.* I don't think so.

I've seen less of Hannity, but there, too, a little goes a long way. I once heard him opine, after several women were molested after the Puerto Rican Day parade, that this would be a lot less likely to happen if more citizens in Central Park were armed. In other words, in

Hannity's worldview a citizen pulling a gun on marauders would compel them to stop. I guess he assumes none of the swarming group is armed. I have a different assumption about the whole thing. More people armed means more people will be shot. Also, Hannity will hold forth with some of the longest question/statements, then when his guest begins to answer shouts over the guest, "Oh, no, you don't!"

I'm happy to watch Brit Hume and others on Fox, and if we measure success by ratings, which we do, then Roger Ailes has done an excellent job building his network. Still, I doubt he'll appreciate what I've had to say about "We report, you decide."

I believe if you do what I do and the occasion presents itself for you to comment on friends who are in public life you must say what you think, or you shouldn't be a commentator. Inevitably there will be hard feelings.

I have been friendly with Warren Beatty for many years. We first met in the movie *Heaven Can Wait*, and over the years we've always enjoyed seeing each other.

When there was conversation about him possibly running for president, I showed a video of an appearance he made at Harvard. Warren had spoken about too much money being in too few people's hands, or words to that effect. Someone in the audience at Harvard asked him if he himself wasn't in that category. Warren is very smart, so I was astonished that he seemed surprised by the question. He never answered it, but instead "did a Warren." He smiled and pointed, and chuckled, and smiled, and nodded, and shrugged and chuckled some more and went to the next question.

Word got back to me that Warren was also "surprised" that his old friend Chuck showed that clip.

Rehired

I'm not exactly sure what Ed Scanlon did or said, but soon I got a call from Andy Lack's colleague David Corvo, saying they wanted me on the weekend. Andy felt I could be more valuable to the company on MSNBC, not CNBC, as they had a greater opportunity there to build their subscriber base, since MSNBC had about 25 million fewer subscriptions. Along with Geraldo, I had earlier been given a lot of credit for building the CNBC subscriber numbers. I can only assume from the call that Andy Lack got the message from Ed Scanlon that not only he but Bob Wright as well would like to see me continue as part of NBC Cable, and while Andy had the final say, maybe this was one he should give to Bob and Ed. The pros outweighed the cons. There were Bob and Ed, they had to pay me anyway, I could help sell subscriptions, and not only that, but the weekend was a hybrid. Maybe someone from "someplace else" like me would be okay there.

So a few weeks after I was fired by NBC, it was announced I was hired by NBC. *Newsweek*'s "Conventional Wisdom" box had fun with it, giving me an up arrow saying, "Loopy, lib actor turned cable pundit, fired, rehired. *Beethoven III* can wait."

When I came back on and asked, "When was the last time somebody was fired and rehired by the same place?" *Time* magazine answered me pointing out that former Yankees manager Billy Martin had been fired and rehired three times by the Yankees. Steve Jobs was fired and rehired twelve years later as CEO of Apple. Then they reached for Richard Burton and Elizabeth Taylor remarrying. Then there was something about Classic Coke coming and going and coming and Grover Cleveland being defeated and then reelected as president. So even if I gave them Billy Martin and Steve Jobs, there was still no one who did it in such a short period of time. I was having fun with it all.

Then late one Sunday night, I saw a car come up my driveway and leave an advance copy of *Newsweek* with a note from the editor saying, "Given the holiday weekend, I wanted to make sure you got an early copy of this week's issue." I was back in business with a much better schedule. The only thing that remained to be seen was the ratings. Were they going to be high enough to justify a renewal after the six months they were obligated to pay me anyway?

In television ratings, news comes very quickly. From the outset the show again was a hit. It was preceded and followed by other public-affairs shows, and it was again, if not the highest rated, then close. Everyone, including Andy Lack, it seemed, was happy.

Six months flew by, and my contract was renewed for another year.

On the last show I did before being canceled on CNBC, Ralph Nader was among the guests. I clearly was making the statement that nothing was going to change by having Ralph on my first show on MSNBC.

I met Ralph Nader long ago through our mutual friend Phil Donahue and sustained a relationship with him over the years. He and his organizations have led the battles for car safety, cleaner air, cleaner water, protecting us from unsafe combinations of medications, and many other issues for public protection. These protections always cost corporations money, so any opportunity to portray him as a radical is seized upon, but without the Ralph Naders of the world, God knows if there's any limit to what some corporations would do to us for their personal gain, including allowing us to be killed.

I particularly remember a case Ralph wrote about in one of his books where an asthma medication caused severe brain damage to a child. The pharmaceutical company knew that under certain circumstances this could happen but chose for financial reasons not to let all doctors know it.

When Ralph Nader told me he was going to run for president, I had misgivings and told him so. While I agree with many of the things Ralph stands for, a run for the presidency then and now seemed a mistake. I really objected during the campaign to his continually saying that there was no difference between the two candidates and their parties. While you can support that in some instances, overall most objective Republicans and Democrats know that's simply not true. It's obvious that Ralph's campaign elected the candidate who least represents his views, and if he runs again he could do it again.

I've heard the argument that America needs a liberal, progressive party, but I don't buy it.

It's clear in our country that unless the far right and the far left work to get their voices heard within their own parties rather than establish their own candidates, all they'll do is elect the other side.

In my opinion, that's the reality and will be in the foreseeable future.

Don Imus

At MSNBC, I began to deal with Don Imus, or the I-Man as he is called by his associates and friends, and all others who are seeking his blessing. This group includes many major politicians and media people, some of whom are my friends.

I have had a checkered experience with Don Imus. I have attacked and praised him on the air, and he's done the same with me. I have been invited to be his guest, which I declined, to his management's amazement: "Doesn't he realize how this exposure will increase his ratings?"

Too often I see Imus and his cohorts as unintentionally (I assume) racist, homophobic, and just plain hateful. I have been saying this for years, and lately that observation is coming more and more from others.

An Imus defense is that others, more extreme than he, are spared these criticisms. The answer, of course, is that others are so low they don't even pretend to be anything but what they are. They don't have major politicians and journalists regularly appearing and are not considered so influential. Obviously when you present yourself as a decent human being, you are held to a different standard.

Also, Imus rationalized, he sometimes has black comics bashing whites on his program and there is no complaint. There seldom is when the majority is attacked. However, for me the most important truth here, which he does not—or refuses to—allow himself to see, is that whatever his intention, he and his program for years have provided an influential venue where negative stereotypes of minorities are regularly reinforced. This has been hurtful and destructive, and no amount of well-publicized good deeds can undo that damage.

A woman sued him recently for ongoing hateful comments about her. This woman had somehow rubbed him the wrong way. The court astonishingly ruled there was no case, saying, in effect, that everyone knew that anything said on talk radio was not meant and surely shouldn't be taken seriously. I wonder how often the judge has listened. Too much of the venom *is* meant and should be taken seriously.

All of this is a shame, because obviously here is a man who has done much good for many important causes. Not only that, he and his colleagues are very talented. Imus, in my opinion, conducts better interviews with newsmakers than some of the people who only do that.

He had a very interesting interview recently with the Pulitzer Prize–winning essayist Tom Friedman of *The New York Times*. Mr. Friedman was describing conditions in China. It was highly informative, and Imus was asking good questions about this country where one-fifth of the world's population lives. The problem was, throughout the interview, I kept thinking how on his show the Chinese people are often referred to as Chinks and Gooks.

Reconciling these two faces of Imus is impossible for me.

He will, I hope, someday see that just because you ridicule yourself, it doesn't give you license to spew ridicule over everyone else, whether they deserve it or not. The self-ridicule gambit was picked up by one of Imus's staff recently. On a promo he referred to himself as a "sickening sycophant." The fact that he called himself that in no way made it easier to listen to him being one. Also, the rationalization by Imus and so many hostile people of "I'm just kidding" is getting old fast.

He got into it once with Judge Harold Rothwax over his feeling that the judge had mistreated his wife as a potential jurist in a case. I'm going to accept that something wrong did happen, as you can't help but notice that once someone puts on those black robes, sits up high, and looks down on you, something arrogant can easily take place. But for weeks Imus went after the judge, attacking him in the most hateful, vicious ways. "Weasel" and "stupid bastard" are two of his favorite expressions. The judge filed a suit, so arguably there could have been grounds, but in the middle of this, the judge suffered a stroke and died. Did any of this abuse contribute to the judge's illness? In my opinion, how could it not? Did it slow the I-Man down? No way!

Imus appears to have venom for friends and foes alike. Here's a man in his sixties who absolutely cannot stop expressing his hostility toward just about every living human being. He then starts a ranch for kids with cancer, putting up large sums of his own money—a complicated man. Even then, he refers to the children afflicted with cancer as "little bastards." That's meant to be humorous as well. Once you mistreat people on a regular basis and, worse yet, being a public personality, inevitably become a role model for others to emulate, there aren't enough ranches in the world you can start to make up for the bad values you've put out there.

However, I must admit I was surprised to find myself enjoying Imus's rude put-down to a woman caller the other day. The woman had appeared to be condescending and all-knowing in her attitude about her subject, old radio personalities, and closed her conversation with a superficial "Have a nice day." The minute she was off the air Imus and his men jumped all over her with mocking "Have a nice day" and other standard Imus insults.

It was clearly inappropriate, but it reminded me of a bunch of kids razzing a stuffed shirt behind his back. Of course, here it was on the air. I still enjoyed it. What I learned from that was that "earned" rude retaliation from Imus is funny. The problem is that 99.9 percent of the time the people don't seem to deserve it. If they do, I haven't heard a good enough reason. He's articulating that rude side most of us properly never express. So he is often inappropriate, which I'm sure is why he's a success.

He is among other things a shock jock. He's expressed his resentment at being referred to that way. Recently I heard him talking to NBC's Dan Abrams about a stay of execution for a man who committed murder when he was seventeen and is now twenty-five. The I-Man thought age shouldn't be an issue. Dan then asked if he thought that if a six-year-old committed murder, he should be executed when he's past the legal age. The I-Man vehemently said he did. Either he meant to shock, or he's insane.

I was listening to a baseball game the other day on the station that broadcasts Imus, and prior to the game they ran a promo for his program. Amid a lot of loud laughter over some joke from which the audience was totally excluded, you could clearly hear "son of a bitch," "motherf——," and "f——." While there was bleeping, it was very clear what was being said, in a promo yet! Obviously there were children listening. If that doesn't violate some regulation, it should!

When the Mars probe failed, costing our space program and country a fortune, it delighted Imus and his minions for days. Why? He himself asked that question. If ever there were candidates for group therapy, it's Don Imus and his associates.

This all blew up in Imus's face when he fired a man named Sid Rosenberg, who was auditioning on the air to be a sports reporter. Rosenberg, I'm sure trying to fit right in, referred to the tennis player Venus Williams, who is African-American, as an "animal" and said she and her sister Serena "have a better shot at posing nude for *National Geographic* than *Playboy.*"

Rosenberg also said, "I can't even watch them play anymore. I find it disgusting. I find both of those, what do you want to call them... They're just too muscular. They're boys." Rosenberg insisted his remarks were not racist. Imus said Rosenberg was fired because his remarks were "not even an attempt to be humorous" but "just moronic."

It seems what Don Imus is saying is that if you mean to be funny, anything goes, including remarks that the I-Man acknowledges are "inappropriate and in poor taste." I assume he means, for example, when it was said on his broadcast of the African-American journalist Gwen Ifill, who was covering the White House for *The New York Times,* "Isn't the *Times* wonderful? It lets the cleaning lady cover the

White House." Mr. Imus clearly makes a significant distinction between "inappropriate and in poor taste" and "moronic," as one is applauded and the other is cause for firing.

Imus is an expert on subtle distinctions. Recently he said, "It's okay to make fun of gay people, but not to be mean to them." It's clear that Imus and not the gay person gets to decide when being made fun of is mean.

So if I understand all of this correctly, if you mean to be funny or maybe even chuckle as you do your thing, you can get away with just about anything. Of course, vicious bullies are known to smirk, grin, and chuckle as they carry out their abuse. If we accept that logic, maybe we need to rethink our feelings about bullies. Not likely.

To use some of Imus's favorite expressions, I think he and his group are "stupid, lying phonies." They really shouldn't be offended by what I've said, because I'm chuckling as I write this.

Following the blowup about the firing of Sid Rosenberg, Imus, in my opinion feeling the heat, decided to "give the kid another chance." I stopped following the saga then, because it all seemed too self-serving and phony. I later heard Sid Rosenberg hosting a sports talk-radio show where he displayed real sensitivity and support to an eleven-year-old caller. It again shows we all have many sides, and it's always a good idea to call on our better ones.

Meanwhile, TomPaine.com published an Imus watch that listed some of the ways the Imus program refers to different minorities. In addition to referring to the Chinese as Chinks and Gooks, blacks were referred to as "gorillas," "pimps," and "knuckle-dragging morons." Gays were called "homo," "lesbo," "load swallowers," and "carpet munchers." That's only a tiny example of what's being presented as humor.

Should Imus be allowed to do this? Clearly the First Amendment protects him, and as far as I can tell, the FCC, which is supposed to oversee programming for children during Imus's broadcast time, appears to see no problem.

The remaining question, again, is how do all the estimable journalists and politicians continue to justify their appearances? For them I would ask two questions. Does this garbage upset minorities? While I'm sure there are exceptions, the answer emphatically is yes. Does it, in the long run, perpetuate negative stereotypes for the next generation, which lead to bigotry, hatred, and sometimes violence? No question, the answer again is yes. Some will have a problem making the jump to violence, but when I ask a gay or black person whether they see a connection between the trash talking and the violence, they say they do. How on earth can these journalists and politicians continue to appear on such a program? I understand some of the journalists are instructed by their networks to be there, but as for the others, one explanation other than self-interest for their appearances is that they are not really aware of what goes on there, which is really hard to believe, or they some how don't see the damage of the "kidding." I have great respect for most of these people, so I just respectfully disagree with their decision to appear.

There could be, however, one other explanation for the appearances of these people: they have the same ambivalence toward Imus that I do and have chosen to appear as I have chosen to sometimes listen. For them, possibly the greater good is served by going on, and for me, at least as far as I'm aware, it's the only place I can consistently hear from all these newsmakers at that time of the day.

President Clinton's most articulate defender in the Monica

mess, James Carville, refers to the president as "a good man who did a bad thing." That's how I see Don Imus. He's a good man who I believe one day will regret at least some of the venom he has elevated to acceptable radio fare and understand that he has significantly contributed to the increasing meanness in the country.

He has done this not only by what he does but, like Howard Stern, by inspiring others going into radio to copy him.

I hope his awareness happens sooner rather than later, so we can all enjoy the talent of Don Imus and his colleagues without wincing.

My daughter told me this story recently. There was some kind of "laugh-off" at a club where any member of the audience could tell a joke. One guy asked, "What's the difference between a piece of pizza and a Jew? A piece of pizza doesn't scream when you put it in an oven." It got some laughs out of the crowd.

Of course, Don Imus and Howard Stern would deplore that joke, but in some instances, that's where this "nothing's off-limits" sensibility toward humor can lead.

It seems a regular occurrence that some radio personality is either fined, suspended, or even fired for some startlingly offensive remark about someone's death. When they are forced to apologize, they always say, "If I offended anyone, in any way, I am truly sorry. That was not my intention. It was an inappropriate attempt to be humorous."

The level of discourse and entertainment is getting more and more vulgar, insensitive, and hateful. I know by far the majority of people in this country deeply object to this.

Civilization, in *every* sense, is worth fighting for.

A Luncheon in Albany

At some point around the time I did my first program from the Bedford Hills Correctional Facility, a young woman by the name of Angela Thompson, who was serving fifteen years to life under the Rockefeller Drug Laws, was granted clemency.

Angela had served eight years. The case for clemency for Angela was spearheaded by a lovely man, a retired judge by the name of Jerome Marx, who had met Angela and taken a personal interest in her case. Angela had no prior record. She got into trouble because she had no place to stay and was taken in by an uncle who unfortunately turned out to be a drug dealer. Eventually he asked Angela to handle a transaction with a man who came to the apartment who was an undercover police officer, and Angela was arrested. Her uncle advised her not to take a plea bargain, so she went to trial and was found guilty.

When I learned of Angela's clemency, I began to wonder if I could do the same for the women I had interviewed at the prison. If clemency was going to be granted, why not for other women who weren't drug dealers, had no prior records, and had small children when sentenced? Also, the four women I had interviewed had already served sentences of nine, eleven, twelve, and seventeen years.

On one of the shows I had done on the Rockefeller Drug Laws, New York State Senator Dale Volker appeared to express support for the laws. The senator was tough, but he was not unreasonable, so I chose to do something after the show that I'd never done before. I called him in his office in Albany and continued our dialogue. Dale Volker acknowledged that there could be certain cases where the law was too harsh for a particular defendant. After several phone calls in which he would make the case for being tough, and I would make the case for being fair as well, which, of course, was Dale's wish, we started to work together to examine cases.

My producer John Gabriel took on the job of planning a lunch in Albany that I would host for about a dozen key senators where I would show video of the women I felt deserved clemency.

John Gabriel is a remarkable producer. I've never met anyone who gets things done more quickly than he does. Over and over I've requested things from John, and five minutes later the phone rings, he tells me it's taken care of, and asks if there's anything else he can do. He's also able to find cameramen who share our sensibility to lower their rate to work within our budget.

After I showed the video to the senators, I asked for questions or comments. One senator said he had watched me on television and said, "If it was up to you, you'd let everyone out of prison." I think he meant it, too. I politely told him he couldn't be further from the truth, that I was just as interested in protecting all of us from criminals as anyone, but that we wanted to be sure we were locking up the right people for long periods of time, which in these cases in my opinion clearly we weren't. The senate leader Joe Bruno seemed to agree with everything I said and promised he would get into it. I gave everyone a copy of the video of the women and drove back to New York hoping for the best.

I then read in the paper about a woman named Katherine Lapp, who represented Governor George Pataki in dealing with these issues. She's the New York State Director of Criminal Justice and the Commissioner of the Department of Criminal Justice Services. With that many titles, you might expect a forbidding person, but when I called her and she agreed to see me, I was very happy to discover a warm person who responded to the video of the women in a manner beyond what I had hoped. We watched it together, and I never once even glanced to check her reaction, because I knew what it would be.

I had exposed the video to all the parties I could who might be helpful in the clemency process, and now it was up to them and their consciences to do the right thing as I saw it, and I believed as they saw it as well.

Leaving the Weekend

In its relatively short history, MSNBC has probably become the cable network that most quickly changes, rearranges, and drops programs. After the war in Kosovo, programming changes began to take place at MSNBC. Quickly, all news-related shows in prime time except mine were either canceled or removed from the weekend. Endless runs and reruns of *Weekend Magazine,* a compilation of *Dateline* pieces, and *Time & Again,* a biography series, filled the weekend hours. The magazine show was hosted by Stone Phillips, and *Time & Again* was hosted by Jane Pauley, who were the two hosts of *Dateline.* (The network believes in getting their money's worth out of their talent and their programs.) The same Brian Williams news broadcast was seen four times a day on CNBC and MSNBC.

There were billboards and TV ads that promoted the newscast with Brian Williams as "the number one rated prime-time newscast." Of course, the ads didn't say it's the *only* newscast in prime time. That's almost as bad as "We report, you decide." I have no an-imus for these people. I know them. I like them. I even like Andy Lack. But you've got to be more straightforward than that.

The reason I have good feelings rather than bad about television executives is simple: There are so few people who provide you an opportunity to do what you do that I ultimately focus on what they've done for me rather than what they haven't. While, like anyone else, I would take note of the bumps, in the big picture I was always grateful I was there at all.

I was now part of a context of magazine pieces and biographies. Instead of following something news related, it would not be unusual for me to be preceded by a biography of Cher or a documentary on roller coasters. It was another version, not as bad, but reminiscent, of my following a rerun of Conan O'Brien.

Soon I was moved to seven o'clock on Friday night, which turned out to be a great hour for cocktail lounges but less so for cable viewing. I held the audience, but the audience was smaller than on the weekend.

I began to think about the other possibilities.

I felt certain I could go to Fox, where Roger Ailes was in charge. Another possibility was the *Today* show. I had met with Jeff Zucker, who ran it, and he was interested in my doing several different kinds of segments for them. Also, my original CNBC producer, Marlene Dann, was now at Court TV, and she was always saying, "Come here and do whatever you want." I also began to consider the possibility of returning to the movies. I did not feel that was compatible with social and political commentary when I began five years ago, but I was very surprised to see a Warren Beatty candidacy for the presidency, of all things, being taken somewhat seriously while he was acting!

So with Fox, Court TV, the *Today* show, and the movies as possibilities, seven o'clock on Friday night on MSNBC seemed less
and less desirable to me.

It was soon clear that the feeling from Andy Lack was mutual.

One day, I was on the phone with Jim Griffin, and he told me
that Chris Matthews, who had been doing his *Hardball* show at
eight on CNBC, was now going to have his original showing at
seven on MSNBC, replacing John Gibson's *Internight* show. I said to
Jim, "Chris's show is on Monday to *Friday* on CNBC, and will now
have its original showing on MSNBC Monday to Thursday. What
about Friday when I'm on?" There was the slightest of pauses before Jim said, "I'll call you right back." Within a few minutes he
called back and said they told him, "Canceling John Gibson in one
week is enough," clearly implying it was only a question of time
before Chris Matthews's show would go from seven o'clock on
Monday through Thursday, to seven on Monday through Friday,
and I would go . . . well, that remained to be seen.

What Next?

Soon it was time to leave. Just as they were when I left CNBC, management was very generous to my staff, offering to find other positions for everyone. Everyone at every level was very friendly from the minute I walked into MSNBC until the day I left. I had formed warm relationships with the on-air people as well as those behind the scenes, particularly the women in the makeup department. I was startled and really touched when more than one woman there actually walked away in tears upon hearing I was leaving.

I went on the air and told the audience I would not disappear but would turn up elsewhere and soon. I mentioned the *Today* show and Court TV, and the movies, and then signed off, saying, "Good night, Mom," for the last time on NBC cable, anyway.

As I left the building after that last show, I was actually very happy. I honestly felt there was nowhere to go but up, and I didn't lack the confidence to think that would happen.

When I was eighteen years old and announced to my parents

that I wanted to become an actor, they were really against it. I remember my mom saying, "No one makes a living doing that."

In Pittsburgh, where I was born and raised, the only person I was
aware of as a teenager that people knew who came out of the area
and became a successful actor was Gene Kelly.

So, "No one makes a living doing that" had a lot of credibility.

I answered by saying, "I'll work harder than other people."

I hope I don't sound too arrogant when I say I feel I did. Today I
would slightly amend that to say that I feel no one worked harder
than I did.

I've thought about this a lot over the years when I've seen really
talented people just kind of disappear from where they were
headed.

I've seen people of notable ability who really don't even think
that much about doing as well as they can. Then there are people
who, in principle, would like to do really well, but don't seem to
have a good idea of what it takes. Then there are those who understand the effort it takes but lack the will to do it. Then there are
people who want to do well, understand what it takes, and have the
will to do it.

Thankfully, I'm in that last category. I've always wanted to do
well at whatever I did. I understood what it took to do it, and I had
plenty of will. To me, like many others, it's not work—I enjoy it.
That's the good news.

I'm not going to list everything about myself that I wish were
different. All right, when you check into a hotel, how much time do
you spend wondering if the blankets are fresh?

It was on a Friday that I left the MSNBC building for the last
time. I felt immediate relief that I was out from under the demand-

ing grind of a weekly show, which, of course, was intended to be a lighter load than the daily schedule, but I had been doing a *Week That Was* type of show and with an all-video, no-guest format, it had not been that different in its demands on me.

Amazingly, on Saturday, only one day later, as I was getting ready to have dinner with a journalist friend, I thought to myself, I miss having my own show! One day after I was glad to be out from under the grind! I decided to call Roger Ailes immediately, set up a meeting, and see about a show at Fox.

My wife and I joined my journalist friend and his wife, and before I had a chance to say I wanted to get a show at Fox, my friend said he'd just been on the phone with Jeff Zucker at the *Today* show, and he was really looking forward to having me on there. I knew Jeff had indicated that to me as well, but that was while I was still with NBC. Now a third person, a highly respected journalist, a booster of mine, was corroborating Jeff Zucker's continuing interest. I said, "How often, every three months?" My friend said, "More like once a month." I said, "Doing what? A mini version of *The Week That Was*?" That idea suddenly seemed too meager—to go from my own show to a monthly five-minute video retrospective. "No," my journalist friend said. "I think we're talking about commentary." That felt entirely different. I quickly did some math in my head. At seven o'clock on Friday night on MSNBC, there was the smallest audience I'd ever had on cable, maybe 150,000 viewers. That's about 600,000 a month, or somewhere over 6 million viewers a year, which is what the audience on the *Today* show could be in one day! I decided to put the Fox idea on hold and called Jim Griffin to set up a meeting with Jeff Zucker at the *Today* show.

Also, sometime in the last few years I had a meeting with the head of CBS News, a man by the name of Andrew Heyward. He was the counterpart to Andy Lack at NBC. Andrew certainly seemed more receptive to me than Andy when I was talking with him and his right-hand man at the time, Jonathan Klein. I remember Jonathan saying to me, "Whenever I'm clicking from channel to channel, I always stop when I come to you." He didn't say how long he stopped when he came to me, just that he stopped, which still sounded pretty good. The meeting was about some participation I might have on their Sunday-morning program *Face the Nation*. While Andrew and Jonathan seemed intrigued by the idea, they ultimately chose not to do it. I believe they felt they would take some probably justifiable complaints from people at the network who'd been there a long time and felt *they* should be on *Face the Nation*.

Jonathan Klein had left the network, but Andrew was still the head of CBS News, and I called him. He was extremely warm, instantly agreed to meet, and even gave me his home phone number if I had to change the appointment. I said to him, "Andy Lack wouldn't even give me his office number," which was kind of what it felt like.

When we met, I again proposed to him that there be a couple of minutes in *Face the Nation* where they go to a kind of a "public citizen" type of person to ask a question and a follow-up. For example, I had seen our then secretary of state, Madeleine Albright, on a Sunday-morning show, responding to reports of a listening device the Russians evidently had placed in the wall of a conference room in our State Department building in Washington. She answered, in effect, that we had spent so much of our resources on securing our embassies all over the world that we didn't really have the money left to shore up the security of our State Department in Washington. She actually said that, and no one seemed all that taken aback by the answer. In fact, they went on to another subject. I suggested filling the role a public citizen would have and asking the question a citizen might ask (which would be, "You've got to be kidding!" I'd say it in a polite journalistic way, of course).

Andrew was intrigued. He kept referring to it as "a very creative idea." He also said just because he felt it was "very creative" didn't mean he was going to do it. I said, "Oh, I don't think you're going to do it. I'm just flattered you're even thinking about it." He then raised some questions: "What about people who say, 'He's an actor'?" He then answered it quickly himself: "Statute of limitations on that one." Mike Wallace had much earlier been an actor as well as a quiz-show host, and that issue had seemed to evaporate. He said, "What about if you come up with a question it was obvious the others should have asked? Won't that be uncomfortable for them?" I said, "Maybe, but anyone on a panel might do that." I told Andrew I was going to be meeting with Jeff Zucker at the *Today* show to see if there was a potential relationship there, and he said that he wanted to think about it and discuss it with the excellent *Face the Nation* host, Bob Schieffer, and that I should call him after the meeting with Jeff Zucker and let him know where that was.

I then called my former producer at CNBC Marlene Dann, who was now at Court TV, and asked her to set up a meeting with Henry Schleiff, who ran the place.

When I showed up for my meeting there were Marlene Dann, Henry Schleiff, and a woman named Sheilah Darcy McGee, a programming executive who stood throughout most of the meeting in obvious pain from a back condition.

I realized as I entered the Court TV building that for the first

time I was in a place that wanted regular advocacy on important social and legal issues. This was the first place where I wouldn't have
to "slip it in."

I had met Henry Schleiff earlier a couple of times, and he too
had said I was welcome to come to Court TV whenever I wanted to
speak out on whatever moved me, so I launched right in on the
Rockefeller Drug Laws. I told the whole saga of how I became
aware of these cruel laws under which a first-time offender can be
sentenced to a mandatory fifteen years to life. I told him how I had
been talking about this on television for years and wanted to continue with "special reports" on Court TV. I said I'd like to interview the children of the women I had interviewed, as the decision
on clemency was nearing. My intention was to send the video of
the children to the powers that be in hopes that would help their
mothers gain clemency. Henry Schleiff is a very bright man who
has the energy as well as the wit you'd expect from a stand-up
comic. He seemed to be so taken with what I had to say that he
leaped to his feet and presented his own version of it, which
frankly I found more compelling than my version. Marlene Dann
sat silently, smiling, taking it all in, and the third executive, Sheilah
Darcy McGee, seemed interested, but clearly preoccupied with
the question of whether her back would hurt less or more if she sat
or stood. I left the meeting under the impression that I was welcome on Court TV whenever I wanted to speak out about whatever I wanted.

A couple of days later on the phone with Jim Griffin, I got a
whole other message. Yes, he said, Henry Schleiff was absolutely
an admirer, but he seemed to be saying to Jim something that
sounded more like if I wanted to be a "guest" on Court TV a few

times a year, that would be great. It sounded like a far cry from a regular contributor with "special reports." I called Marlene Dann and basically got the same message. I asked Marlene, who by now was a good friend, if she hadn't gotten a different impression at the meeting. She said she had, but then told me it was really an issue of what I would cost.

So now MSNBC was gone, the *Today* show was certainly not a sure thing, nor, of course, was *Face the Nation* that likely, and Court TV seemed to be going away. I immediately called Henry and said, "I get the impression you'd really like to have me on Court TV, but money is an issue." He said, "Look, I won't go into a long thing right now of what a fan I am of yours, but, yes, you're right, money is an issue." I said, "How about I work for nothing?" He said, "Nothing!" I said, "I'm not interested in making money talking about our justice system. I just want the venue. I'll need a thousand total per report for my producer and a cameraman." He quickly said, "A thousand dollars? Sold! Say no more!"

So I could be on Court TV the way I originally intended. As far as making a living, I felt, well, I'd have to find some other way to do that.

Next I wanted to determine how real the *Today* show opportunity was. When I earlier referred to it as not a sure thing, it reminded me of an exchange I'd had years ago with a Hollywood producing team by the name of Arlene Sellars and Alex Winetsky. They had backed many movies, including the Goldie Hawn picture *Private Benjamin*. I had read them a screenplay I had written for which I was trying to get financing. After I finished the reading, they said, "We're going to do your movie." About two weeks later, I heard they weren't going to do it. I called and spoke to Alex. I said,

"I thought you said you were going to do my movie?" He said, "When we said we were going to do your movie, that didn't mean we were going to do your movie." I said, "It didn't? What did it mean?" "It meant," he said, "we were going to do your movie if Warner Bros. wanted to distribute it." There were about three more *ifs* after that, but after the first one, I kind of stopped listening. So even though Jeff Zucker had said he'd like to have me on the *Today* show I really wasn't sure if "I want you on the *Today* show" meant "I want you on the *Today* show." Nobody ever said this stuff was easy.

I showed up at the *Today* show offices and was asked to take a seat until Jeff finished a staff meeting. The seat was an upholstered bench with no back, and as I sat there awkwardly trying not to slouch, I was thinking how here was a good example of aesthetics (in someone's opinion) winning out over practicality. Surely a good-looking bench with a back could have been found. Maybe I thought about these things to avoid thinking about the awkwardness of where I was, and what I was doing.

Leaving the movies to enter the world of television, I had gone from being paid large sums of money and never being anywhere except where people were happy to get me, to working for nothing on Court TV and trying not to slouch on a bench waiting to see if the *Today* show was interested, probably also for no salary. Why? I had become an advocate for people who needed one, and that seemed to transcend every other consideration. It wasn't a plan. It was just the way it was, and I felt privileged and was very happy with the turn of events.

After about ten minutes during which I tried to maintain an acceptable posture, Jeff Zucker's assistant appeared again to tell me he was caught up in this staff meeting but would like me to come in and join it. Hmm, I thought, as I walked toward Jeff's office. Maybe "I want you on the *Today* show" does mean he wants me on the *Today* show.

As I entered Jeff's office, he was sitting behind his desk and there were a half-dozen producers sitting around the large office with pens poised over pads. Jeff didn't introduce me to anyone, but immediately asked me how I would cover the story of the six-year-old Cuban boy Elian Gonzalez. This was prior to New Year's Eve, and it had been recently reported that New York's Mayor Giuliani was going to invite the boy to participate in the ball-dropping ceremony. All the major politicians had weighed in with their opinions, and the boy seemed to be constantly on television, so when Jeff asked me with what angle I would approach the story, I said, "Child abuse." I didn't think that seemed all that inspired. It seemed obvious to me that everyone was exploiting this boy for political gain, but evidently it had not been discussed, as everyone at Jeff's direction began to try to figure out who would ask the mayor about abuse. Jeff then asked me if I was going to do *Beethoven III*, and I said, "It depends how this meeting goes." Everyone laughed as their meeting adjourned and Jeff came over to sit near me.

I told him I had three ideas. One (I liked the least) could be a mini version of *The Week That Was* we had earlier discussed. Another would be advocacy pieces such as focusing on the Rockefeller Drug Laws. The third would be straight commentary. He quickly said he liked the advocacy idea, and was "intrigued" by the commentary. Jeff is in the steel-trap-mind category. He doesn't say much. He gets right to the point, says what he has to say, and that's that. He said he would get me a date in January to show video of the women inmates and discuss the Rockefeller Drug Laws. I then told him about my relationship with Andrew Heyward and the possibility of being part of *Face the Nation*. I told him I had said I would call Andrew after meeting with him first to see if we could have a relationship. Jeff quickly said, "We can have a relationship. I can't put you on every week, but I can put you on every month." As he walked me out of his office, he said, "You don't have to do *Beethoven III.*" It seemed now I could be on the *Today* show every month with its audience of 6 million, and Court TV whenever I wanted to, which had a somewhat larger audience than MSNBC. These were attractive, available venues without the responsibility of a very demanding weekly show. I drove home feeling pretty good.

Movies

I'm always aware of what a fortunate position I'm in profession-
ally that one of my fallback positions is to return to the movies.

A meeting had been set up for me with a top executive at a film
company in New York. This was the first time in about seven years
I'd had anything to do with the movies, and the executive greeted
me like a lost legend of the silver screen. "Charles Grodin, what an
honor! Thank you so much for coming here. Charles Grodin is sitting in my office!" Even I was starting to get excited that Charles
Grodin was there. It reminded me of the director Joel Schumacher,
who directed Lily Tomlin and me in *The Incredible Shrinking Woman*.
He used to say, "I'm giving directions to Lily Tomlin and Charles
Grodin, and they're listening to me!"

The guy all but lifted me on his shoulders. I told him that while
I might be interested in coming back to the movies, I wasn't interested in traveling anywhere (which, believe me, is more than a
slightly limiting statement). It didn't faze him at all. He promised
to inquire about studio facilities in Connecticut, which is my home
state. He even suggested looking into converting some space into a

studio near my home, if only that could lure me back. He expressed his enthusiasm in various ways for about an hour.

After the meeting, I never heard from him again.

I've been to a lot of locations in the course of a thirty-year career in the movies, and it's obvious that others welcomed the opportunity for travel more than I have.

I'm not proud to say that I seemed to appreciate the men diving off the cliffs in Acapulco about as much on television as I did when I saw them in person.

I did, however, find it amazing to witness full daylight at 10 P.M. in Montana in the summer, and there were a few situations that came out of my traveling to other countries that I think about to this day.

I'm not sure what it says about me that it's the "situations" I think about more than the beauty of the different countries. It probably means I live in my head more than most, which has clearly been a liability as well as an asset.

I remember flying to Morocco, which is one country away from Libya, at a time when we were going at it hot and heavy with their leader, Muammar Qaddafi. We flew through the night to Marrakesh. Also on the flight was an executive from the studio. Being pretty aware of my own capabilities or lack thereof, I knew I'd never sleep on this flight without some help, so I planned to take 5 milligrams of Valium at a certain point.

I was talking with the movie executive for the first hour or so of the flight, and at some point I discreetly took the Valium. Since I almost never use the stuff, I have no immunity to it, so I knew it would work. After about twenty minutes, I said to him, "Well, if you'll excuse me, I think I'll get some sleep," and promptly did.

This executive, not a particularly relaxed flyer, never stopped talking to everyone about how cool I was that when I decided to go to sleep, I just went to sleep.

I never told anyone about the Valium. I figure if people think you're cool, let them think you're cool.

I also vividly remember while filming in Morocco being in a helicopter above the presidential palace. Evidently there was an understanding with palace officials that we would only be above the palace for a limited number of minutes.

Some countries are always more or less under siege from dissidents, and the palace guard really didn't want an American movie company's helicopter, or anyone else's for that matter, getting a bird's-eye view of the castle's fortifications.

In the movies, as in the construction business, everything takes longer than planned, so we were up there in that helicopter above the palace waiting for someone to say "Action" longer than agreed. As more and more armed guards began to stare up at us, the helicopter pilot thought it would be a good idea to get the hell out of there right away. I heartily agreed.

In the early 1970s I remember being at Oxford, outside of London, shooting the movie *11 Harrowhouse.*

One night I was in one of those restaurants where the tables are so close together it's as though you're actually having dinner with the people on either side of you.

To my right was a middle-aged couple, and to my left was a mother with her daughter in her twenties. When my food arrived, I did something, oddly enough, I don't remember ever doing before or since. I sent it back and ordered something else. The man to my right asked me what the problem was. I said, "It had way too much fat and gristle. Why do you ask?" He said, "I've ordered the same thing."

I then struck up a conversation with the lady and her daughter to my left, who had seen me in the movies and were very flattering. After about ten minutes, I heard the man to my right say, "I don't know how good an actor you are, but you sure know lousy food."

In the middle of filming the movie *Sunburn* in Mexico, I became friendly with a young Mexican woman working on the picture. One day I asked her if she'd like to have dinner sometime. She said that she'd love to, but she didn't want to see me hurt. I asked, "Hurt? How do you mean?" She said that she had been dating a man who was very jealous and possessive, and she recently broke it off when she learned he was married. I said, "Wait a minute. He's married. You broke up with him, and he's jealous of anyone *you* date?" She said, "Yes. He's a very high-ranking police official and he has a vi-olent temper, and that could be very bad for anyone I went out with."

In truth, right there I wanted to get on a flight to the States im-mediately, but I was playing a heroic figure in the movie, and I had an image to uphold, so I said, "I'm not worried about him. If you want to have dinner with me, we'll have dinner."

A few nights later we did, but I got her to bring along her sister.

I don't want you to get the impression I'm not a tough guy or anything, but about nine years earlier, when I was also in Mexico making the movie *Catch-22,* some of our people were out on the town and had a run-in with some local men. One of the Mexican policemen who was assigned to keep an eye on us asked, "You want us to kill them?"

In any case, shortly after the meeting with the studio guy who never called again, movie offers began to come in from elsewhere. The first one came with the message, "You can write your own ticket." It was very flattering, until I read the script. The character was despicable, a liar, a cheat, a blackmailer. The next one was a homophobic racist. "Sharon Stone would play your wife," they said. "Thanks, but no thanks," I said. It's true that years ago, before *Midnight Run* and the *Beethoven* movies, I had played some jerks—*Heaven Can Wait* comes to mind—but there's a big difference between playing a jerk and playing a funny jerk. I hoped these casting ideas were coming from my early movie work and not my recent television hosting. The offers continued to come, but nothing really got my interest.

Then I received a call that held real promise. It was from a fellow named Michael Chinich, who had been the casting director on *Midnight Run* and after that had gone to work for Ivan Reitman, who produced the two *Beethoven* movies and *Dave*, which I had done. He said, "We've been talking about you and would love to work with you again. We've worked with you three times and had three hits and we really love the experience as well." I said that I felt the same way, but I was involved with some discussions at a television network that might not allow me to do movies, and I would know soon and let them know.

60 Minutes II

The discussion at the network I was referring to was precipitated by a conversation I had on the phone with a friend in the media. He said, "Why don't you look into the *60 Minutes II* situation?" I knew that there was another version of *60 Minutes* during the week, but I had no idea what he meant.

Evidently, *60 Minutes II* was considering replacing the fellow in the Andy Rooney slot on their program, and my friend thought it was a natural for me. He said, "Why don't you have your agent look into it?" Then he quickly said, "No, wait, let me make a call." Five minutes later he phoned to say the fellow in charge of the show, Jeff Fager, seemed receptive to the idea and wanted to see some video on me that might be relevant. "This could work," he told my friend. Ten minutes after that, Jim Griffin was on the phone telling me he had just received a call from Jeff Fager asking to see some tape. I sent some appropriate material on to Jim, who sent it to Jeff. A few days later, Jim called to say Jeff really liked what he saw, wanted to see more, and asked for copies of all my books. Things were looking promising. Obviously, the excellence of the *60 Minutes* franchise and the enormous audience made this an outstanding oppor-tunity. The *Today* show was a huge step up from MSNBC, but *60 Minutes II*, or *62* as they called it, had more than twice the audience of the *Today* show, and it was every week, not once a month.

A couple of weeks went by and a meeting was arranged for me to meet Jeff Fager. Every time I've entered a CBS building, I can't help but remember my "unusual" first experience with this net-work.

When I first arrived in New York in the 1950s, I became friends with a wonderful actress named Eleni Kiamos. Eleni was one of two close friends who died prematurely because they didn't believe in seeing doctors. While still living in Pittsburgh, I had seen her on the highly regarded *Studio One* television program. Eleni and I were in the same acting class with Uta Hagen. She was a truly gifted young actress and was responsible for three very important intro-ductions at the beginning of my career, which, of course, is the time when it's virtually impossible to meet anyone. First she intro-duced me to a woman named Joan Horvath, who gave me the star-ring role in an off-off-Broadway show. It paid no salary, but a review of the play led to my first agent. Later she introduced me to the legendary acting teacher Lee Strasberg, which led to my being accepted as his student. And then she introduced me to a casting director at CBS who began to use me in the Sunday-morning dra-mas *Look Up and Live, Lamp Unto My Feet,* and *Camera Three*. It was my first foot in the door in television.

On one of these shows something happened that I found dis-turbing. A cast of around sixteen was hired, and after the first read-ing around a table at CBS, about six people were told their services wouldn't be required. They were given twenty-five dollars each and sent on their way. This wasn't because the producer didn't like them. It was just that a decision was made that those roles weren't necessary, and it was a way to cut the budget. It all struck me as too whimsical and hurtful. I made my feelings known to Eleni's friend, the casting director, who told me it was done all the time. Even though these Sunday-morning shows were my only source of employment, I pursued what I saw as inappropriate behavior. Of course, the casting director was annoyed, to put it mildly. She pointed out that I was one of the people who was kept, not dismissed. I said that really wasn't relevant. I just felt something wrong was taking place, and unless these people were rehired, I would take this to the union. She said that if I forced them to rehire the people, they would do it, but that I'd never work there again.

The people were rehired, and I never worked there again.

Now here it was, forty years later, and I was entering a CBS building directly across the street from my first encounter. I think in no small part I owe my whole career to my ability to outlast those who would like to see me go away.

I took the elevator to the *60 Minutes* offices, announced myself at the reception desk, and was asked to take a seat. After about ten minutes, I was taken back to an area outside of Jeff Fager's office where I waited a little while longer. Since I was being considered to replace someone, I was a little uncomfortable being observed there.

Jeff appeared after about five minutes and greeted me with what I felt was unusual warmth. We spent about an hour together. He was very complimentary about the tapes he'd seen and my books, and said, "You're on the top of the list." Later, I remembered another time I was told I was number one on a list, and the guy who was number three was chosen.

Jeff asked if I would be willing to do a few pieces for them designed exactly for the spot. I said I'd be happy to, and he said he'd assign a producer. I told him I'd write some pieces and come back next week to present them to him.

The following week, we met again. This time as I was waiting to see him, I ran into Morley Safer and Charlie Rose, who works with *60 Minutes II*. I've known both of them for years, but neither asked why I was there. Even so, I was uncomfortable.

I didn't know the fellow whom they were considering replacing, but I've been replaced twice as an actor and, of course, it's about anyone's least favorite thing.

When Jeff and I were alone in his office, I read him ten pieces I had written. He seemed genuinely enthusiastic about seven of them, so much so that when I left, he handed me a *60 Minutes II* pen. I was feeling pretty optimistic. Later I had dinner with Regis Philbin and told him all about what was going on and for fun showed him the pen as proof. Regis feigned disbelief and joked, "Anyone could get their hands on one of those."

About two weeks after that, Jeff Fager had taken over a suite at the Plaza Hotel, and with a full crew we put five pieces on tape. They sent me a copy a few days later with the *60 Minutes II* clock ticking after each spot, and a note from Jeff saying he thought they came out very well and he'd talk to me next week. At the end of the next week, I got a message from his associate who had produced the pieces, saying that Jeff was away and would be in touch the following week. In the meantime, I went to Kansas City with my wife and son to visit my mother-in-law for Christmas.

Clemency

It was 5 A.M., December 24, 1999, the morning of Christmas Eve, and I couldn't sleep. I'd been awake on and off throughout the night. I had received some news late in the afternoon the previous day that I'd been waiting and hoping for for some time now, and it was what kept me awake.

Three of the four women for whom I had sought clemency had received it from New York Governor George Pataki. They would most likely be released from prison in a few weeks. Combined, they had at least sixteen more years to serve, and even then there was no guarantee they'd be out. As I have said, they were all young mothers who had never been in trouble with the law prior to this time. They had seven children among them. Arlene Oberg, one of the sweetest women I've ever met, was a drug addict who was pregnant when arrested. She took orders for a dealer to support her habit. Her daughter Lisa was born in prison. Her three-year-old, Stephanie, was taken away by her husband, and Arlene's existence is kept from Stephanie, as is her sister Lisa's existence. Arlene could have had a three-year plea bargain, but what ended up being bad advice from her attorney got her a mandatory sentence of twenty years to life, of which she had served eleven years, until she was granted clemency.

Jan Warren wanted to get out of a bad relationship with a man who dealt drugs. She was living on the East Coast and wanted to move back West, but had no money. Her cousin asked her if she could get some cocaine for a friend, and Jan for the first time in her life agreed to bring it upstate herself to get the money to get away from her personal situation. Unknown to her cousin, who was doing it for a "friend," it was a police setup. Jan's personal situation now became a mandatory sentence of fifteen years to life. She had never been in trouble with the law before. She had served twelve years prior to being granted clemency.

Elaine Bartlett, the third woman who received clemency, had served seventeen years of a twenty-to-life sentence. She was on welfare, the mother of four small children, and had never been in trouble with the law before. She was working in a beauty parlor when a "friend" told her she could make two thousand dollars if she delivered four ounces of cocaine to someone in upstate New York. It too was a setup, and Elaine had been in prison from the age of twenty-six to forty-three. When she was arrested, she had five dollars in her pocket. All this is in the land of the Rockefeller Drug Laws. Not one of these women had fully grasped the possible consequences of what she was doing.

We're talking about first-time offenders, addicts, messengers, desperate poor young mothers whom we're locking up for huge portions of their lives while their babies suffer and real drug dealers remain free! It's considered okay for police to pay someone to entrap a mother of four small children who's on welfare and send her to prison for twenty years to life. In America! We separate a mother from her children for seventeen years for being a courier, and we're always talking about family values?

Earlier I had done interviews on Court TV with the son of Elaine Bartlett and the daughter of Arlene Oberg, which I had sent on to the powers that be in Albany.

Robert Bartlett said that he had tried to lead his life in a way that would honor his mother. Lisa Oberg said that when her mommy came home she would give her the bedroom, because she really liked the sofa bed.

I found these young people so compelling, and from what I was told, the people in Albany did as well.

On Wednesday, January 26, 2000, Elaine Bartlett, Arlene Oberg, and Jan Warren were released from prison. I drove into New York to a restaurant in Greenwich Village so I could personally greet them. As I approached the restaurant, I saw Elaine Bartlett standing on the sidewalk. It was thrilling just to look at her. She was free. There was a lot of media there. Every moment was recorded. When an interviewer asked me the simple question "How do you feel?" I found myself unable to speak. The emotion just overwhelmed me. To see these women there in the restaurant, hugging their children, when I had seen them only in prison before, had to be one of the most gratifying events of my life.

We have allowed a huge underclass in our country to remain subjugated, surrounded by drugs, crime, and lack of education, and therefore deprived of job opportunities to escape these environments. We put waste outlets in these areas that cause high percentages of deadly asthma in children, and we entrap poor people and then lock them up for large portions of their lives and say, "We're

Lisa Oberg and Robert Bartlett shortly before their moms received clemency.

With Elaine Bartlett (top), Jan Warren (above), and Arlene Oberg (left), who served a total of forty years in prison because of the cruel Rockefeller Drug Laws. That's Arlene's mother hugging her. She raised her granddaughter while Arlene was in prison and recently died.

tough on crime!" I call it something else. I say we're short on brains and heart. With all our political leaders telling us how religious they are, it begs the question they are always raising: What, indeed, would Jesus say?

The day after the party, I was on the *Today* show in New York. I was on for five and a half minutes talking about the women and some of the cruel laws we have in America. The following couple of days, the potential impact of the *Today* show was clear, as several people I encountered had seen the show. I couldn't help but wonder again at the potential of *60 Minutes II*.

It has been clear in my brief encounters with political leaders that the fact that I am not a paid lobbyist, and that in fact I'm not paid by anyone for anything regarding these issues, has encouraged people to be responsive to me. Also, the political leaders know I could easily turn up later talking on television or being interviewed in newspapers on these issues, which doesn't hurt my access. Also, there's the implication that if the talk gets too heavy, they can always ask me, "What's David Letterman really like?"

Replacing Someone?

A few weeks after taping five sample pieces for *60 Minutes II*, I received an enthusiastic call from Jeff Fager, who said he could have put all five pieces on the air. I told him of other ideas I had, and he quickly said, "Let's do them." It was starting to remind me of the time I was being considered for the role in *Midnight Run*. I spent several hours on several days auditioning with Robert De Niro for the director. It couldn't have gone better, and yet after it was all over, the director called me from an airplane to arrange another audition. I asked what he would like to see that he hadn't seen. It was something about "more something." The static on the line prevented my hearing what he said. Finally I told my agent, as a strategic move, that before I flew to Los Angeles to audition again, "Let's make sure we can make a deal," and then asked for more money than they intended to pay. The director called back and said, "Would you take less if we forget about more auditions?" I said, "Yes," and we quickly made a deal.

In the *60 Minutes II* situation, it wasn't a money issue, but I couldn't figure out what the issue was. I broached the subject by kidding around: "I know Mickey Rooney is your first choice, but what's the plan here?" This, of course, was code for "What's actually happening?" He said he didn't want to go forward with any reservations. Even though it was awkward I asked, "What are your reservations about me?" He said he didn't have any. The reservations had to do with being absolutely sure they intended to replace the other fellow, to give him every chance. I had reason to empathize.

One of the most hurtful events of my professional life happened when I was replaced in an off-Broadway play called *Steambath* in 1971. I had recommended the movie star Anthony Perkins as director. I had become friends with Tony when we did the movie *Catch-22* together, and one of the producers of the play was my old friend Dick Scanga, who was the closest thing to a mentor I'd ever had when I was beginning. I told Dick that while Tony had never directed, he was very bright and had excellent taste. Tony got the job, and the star of the play was the late Dick Shawn. After a while, Dick was replaced by that excellent actor Rip Torn, but then Rip was let go, and I was asked to come in. By now, previews had been extended and Tony Perkins was off in Hollywood fulfilling a previous commitment in a movie, and another director, Jacques Levy, was temporarily in charge. Since Dick Shawn and Rip Torn were a lot more well known than I was at the time, I accepted with some trepidation.

I went into the play with very little rehearsal, but soon the audience response got stronger and stronger. The lead producer, a man named David Balding, and the writer, Bruce Jay Friedman, saw that the play was working better and must have assumed it had little to do with me. They felt what was really needed was a marquee name to make up for all the money lost in delaying the opening. And who better than Tony Perkins, who was soon becoming available? Against the advice of my friend Dick Scanga, and the writer Bruce Friedman's sons, they replaced me. The thing I did best in life at that point was act, and I felt it was probably one of the most appropriate roles for me I'd ever had, so you might imagine how I felt. For weeks I had nightmares about being replaced. Given my instinct for survival, I later wrote a play about someone being replaced that had a run in New York and got an excellent review in the *Times*. The following year Bruce Friedman came into Dick Scanga's office and said, "They're making a movie out of a story I wrote and guess who the star is?" Dick, who already knew, said, "Charles Grodin." That was *The Heartbreak Kid*.

Even though I think it's an outstanding piece of work, *Steambath* opened to mixed to poor reviews. The critics felt Tony Perkins was miscast, and the play closed after a short run.

About twenty-five years later, they were considering doing a revival of the play in New York and wanted to do a reading of it in a Broadway house, and the producer called me of all people to read the leading role, which I did. The reading went very well.

Unfortunately, the whole experience ended my friendship with Tony Perkins, who was a bright, fun, terrific person who's now passed away.

So I understood the pain of being replaced, and while I still didn't know what would happen with *60 Minutes II*, I felt if I did end up with the job, I would regret that someone had to lose the position in order for me to have it.

David Letterman

I usually have the phones turned off by 9 P.M. but one night I didn't, and I got a call from the producer of the David Letterman show, a fellow by the name of Rob Burnett.

David had recently undergone bypass surgery and the show had been in reruns. Beginning the following week, they were going to try something different. They would have a host sit on the steps of the stage of the Ed Sullivan Theater and chat with other friends of the show, and then show outstanding clips of the guest's previous appearances. This was sort of a hybrid guest-host position. Of course, I was flattered to be asked to do it for the first night. The guest for the front half of the show would be Julia Roberts and the second half guest would be Regis Philbin.

I went to New York to do it. It would be the first time I had seen Julia Roberts in eleven years, since we had screen tested together for the movie *Pretty Woman*. Clearly she had gotten the role and I hadn't, but there was a little more to it than that. The picture was being made by Disney, and I had been told by a Disney executive about a week after the screen test that when Michael Eisner, who runs the whole Disney operation, saw the test he said, "Get Charles Grodin for the role." He was told Richard Gere had already been signed (Richard hadn't tested, and I think it's okay to tell this story now since the picture was such a huge hit with Julia and Richard).

I didn't give the whole thing much thought until years later, when I was hosting my show on CNBC and had the director of the picture, Garry Marshall, as a guest. He began talking about *Pretty Woman* on camera with me and casually said Richard Gere had been signed for the picture "before" I flew out to test, that I was brought in to "draw out comedy in Julia." If I'd known that at the time, of course, I wouldn't have flown out.

So here I was seeing Julia for the first time in eleven years. As we hugged, I whispered into her ear, "I guess you got the part." She quietly said, "Yes." That was the last quiet thing about her. For the next thirty minutes or so, she was funny, smart, charming, and everything else you'd want someone to be. I was thinking, if they pay anyone twenty million dollars a picture, who better than she? In our exchanges between clips of Julia's past appearances on the show, she took the tack that she adored Dave, which I believe she did, and I took the position that he didn't even have bypass surgery, that it was all a PR stunt. I said a friend of mine had seen him at a club recently at 3 A.M. doing the hully-gully. It was a lot of fun, as it was also with my friend Regis.

When Regis Philbin is in your life, you get to see two distinct personalities. Off camera he is quiet, sensitive, kind, but of course, still a lot of fun.

The Regis you see on camera, who seems always to be in various entertaining degrees of outrage, is the one who used to come to guest on my show.

Thankfully, Dave always knows I'm joking.

When he appeared with me, the comic complaints began the minute he entered the building and continued on the elevator, in the makeup room, on the air, and even during the commercial breaks. The whole building was laughing as Regis carried on with the various "handles" to each complaint. "I can't believe"; "Will you look at this guy?"; "How can it be?"

Regis never stopped until he left the building—which could easily be a couple of hours. There are two possible ways to look at this. The man has an inexhaustible supply of comic energy, or maybe a lot of things really do bug him!

Sometime later, after Dave returned to the show, I got an unusual invitation to come back in what was referred to as a "celebrity cameo" for a "new for ratings period segment." The idea was for Dave to introduce new concepts for the sweeps period. Sweeps, for those of you who may not know, are ratings periods during which advertising rates are determined. One of Dave's ideas to boost ratings for this period would be to have a red panic button on the side of his desk. According to the idea as presented to me in a letter referred to as a "formal invitation," when there would be a lull in the show, Dave would press the panic button and I would be lowered down from the rafters into the guest chair as an "instant guest." I would begin to tell an anecdote and then be raised back up to the rafters as Dave said, "We look forward to seeing you all through sweeps, Chuck."

While I was flattered by the invitation's suggestion that I would be an instant boost to ratings (or maybe anyone lowered from the ceiling to guest would be), it somehow didn't fit the potential *60 Minutes* profile. If I'd still been on cable, I might have done it. Maybe.

I've had great times with David Letterman over the years. My favorite has to be when I brought my "attorney" on with me to threaten a lawsuit.

I didn't personally see this, because I keep early hours, but someone told me that twice in one week Dave had guests with whom my name came up, and he or the guests "went after me."

The guests were, on one night, Carol Burnett, and another the acerbic Dabney Coleman—both close friends of mine.

I asked to see the tapes of the show, then called Dave's producer and told him I wanted to come on for an elaborate lawsuit bit, bringing the old vaudevillian Joey Faye with me as my attorney.

What follows is the text of what happened.

Dave (talking to camera): Certain remarks were made on this program regarding our first guest. Because of our usually good relationship with this man, Mr. Grodin, we have decided to invite
  him back here tonight to discuss this with us. Ladies and gentle-
  men, here he is, Charles Grodin.
*(I enter looking very unhappy and refuse to shake David's outstretched
hand.)*
Dave: Charles, welcome to the show. I understand . . .
Me (jumping in): You keep saying you don't know why I'm here, but
  you do know why I'm here!
Dave (incredulous): What is it?
Me: Last week on two separate nights, one with Carol Burnett, and
  one with Dabney Coleman, I was really libeled on the show.
Dave (all innocence): Oh . . . how so?
Me: Well, certain things were allowed to go out on the air . . .
Dave: Right.

Me:...that were said about me. You said certain things and Dabney
   Coleman said certain things that were allowed to go out on the air.

Dave: But it's just a joke, and I can't...Are you serious about this?

Me: Well, I don't think it's a joke.

Dave: You're really actually serious?

Me: I don't think it's a joke, and I think when the audience sees the
   tape of the previous shows, they will see that it's not that clearly
   a joke. In fact, I've brought with me tonight my attorney, who's
   going to sit here with me, so Neal Fraymens is my attorney, and
   I'd like to bring him out. Neal? Neal?

*(Joey Faye enters, a short older man dressed in a dark blue suit and looking
very somber.)*

I believe most people in the audience who weren't sure if this
was a joke now became sure.

Dave (grinning): Neal, nice to see you. How are you?

(Joey shakes Dave's hand while I look displeased.)

Me: Neal is the senior partner of Fraymens and Llewelyn, and
   uh...Why don't you show the audience what I saw last Wednesday and Thursday....

Dave: I have not seen the videotape....

Me (jumping in): But you were here when it happened!

Dave: Yes, I was here, but I don't, don't...but I understand our director and our producer have put this together, and...

Me: This is actually what happened last week on the show.

Dave: I don't think this is actionable but... (*To the director:*) Go
   ahead, Hal, roll that videotape if you have it.

(Video comes on of Dave with Carol Burnett.)

Dave: You know who was here a couple of weeks ago, and we had all kinds of trouble with him?

Carol: Who's that?

Dave: A very nice guy, and a man for whom I have the highest regard as an actor and really a decent fellow. Charles Grodin.

Carol: Chuck? Yeah. He is quite a friendly person. I understand he doesn't behave that way sometimes on talk shows....

Dave: We have trouble with Chuck. We have trouble with him, y'know, because he's psychotic.

(The video cuts to Dave with Dabney Coleman.)

Dabney: Chuck Grodin. That pain in the ass.

Dave: He's a very nice man.

Dabney: Oh God. He's nice if you talk about him, but if you get off of him for a second, whoa! He resents that. He takes that personally.

Dave: I get the sense that the two of you would be a great combination.

Dabney: He thinks so too. I don't.

(We come back to Dave and Joey and me.)

Me: Not only that, but there was more than that....

Dave: What's the other part?

Me: Well, you also said I would die if anyone ever touched me. Let me ask you something....

Dave: It's just a joke.

Me: Yeah, well, it doesn't look like a joke. I'll tell you the truth. You say I would die if anyone even touched me. Are you married?

Dave: Uh, no.

Me: I am married. Do you have any children? No! I have two children. Do you get massages? I get massages regularly.

(Joey leans in and whispers something in my ear.)

Dave: Oh. Oh.

Me (to Joey): Are you chewing gum?

(Joey shakes his head no and continues to whisper as I look increasingly unhappy.)

Dave: What is it?

Me: My attorney would like a glass of water.

Dave: Oh yeah. *(Dave reaches down and picks up a pitcher.)* We have some water here. *(Dave pours a glass of water for Joey as Joey walks over to Dave's desk.)*

Joey: Thank you very much. Listen, I enjoy your show.

Me (to Dave): You also ... you also ...

(Joey stands there drinking, as I stare at him.)

Dave: You want me to freshen that up for you?

Joey: No. No.

Me (after a long disdainful look at Joey): You also talked about the Friendly movement that Carol and I started, and you said you thought it was a joke.

Dave: I did. I think it's a joke.

Me: You couldn't believe that somebody like me would be out there saying people should be more friendly?

Dave: Should be more friendly. Right.

Me: You really did think that was a joke?

Dave: I still think it's a joke.

Me: It was not ...

(Joey taps me on the shoulder, leans in to whisper to me again, but instead fakes a huge sneeze on my shoulder that looks completely real. I recoil in disgust. Dave stands and hands some tissues to Joey, who takes them and sneezes on me again.)

Me: Oh! This is ridiculous! You don't get an attorney from the Yellow Pages. I don't care what anyone says! Look, I'll tell you what. This is serious to me. *(Stares at Joey.)* This guy is... Look, we're not going to handle this tonight! We'll handle this in court! (*To Joey, as I walk off.*) You're friendly with him. *You* sit with him!

Dave: Charles! Aw! *(A silence.)* Gee, that's... that's... kind of ugly.

(Joey walks over to Dave.)

Joey: Y'know, he *is* psychotic.

Dave: I think you may be right.

(Joey walks off as Dave laughs.)

Of course, Joey Faye's ability to do a very realistic sneeze certainly had everything to do with the sequence working.

After that broadcast, Dave's producer, Bob Morton, and I had lunch at the Friars Club with another older comic in an effort to persuade him to do one of his specialty bits with me on Dave's show.

The idea was that I would come on and say to Dave that I was concerned that my appearances with him weren't really in my best interests, as I always seemed to be complaining. I would then add that my press agent particularly was unhappy that I appeared here, and that he was watching nervously in the green room right now.

At that point Dave would say, "Well, let's get him out here to discuss this." The comic would then come out, take a seat, begin to make his point, and as he did, one by one, his teeth would start to fall out. (He did this by holding Chiclets gum in his cheeks.)

At lunch the comic listened carefully to our proposal, but declined, saying he didn't want to appear as "a stooge." To me, he'd be the funny one in the appearance, but of course we respected his feelings.

As the lunch came to an end he said to me, "I'd really like to work with you sometime. See if you can come up with something for me."

I'm sorry he chose not to do it, because I think it would have been hilarious with Dave and me scurrying around picking his "teeth" up off the floor as he held forth.

Speaking Up

While I continued to wait to hear from Jeff Fager, I went on vacation with my wife and son and something unusual happened. I assume it's more than obvious by now that I'm one of those people who feel an obligation to say something if I see something wrong. Some people view people like me as admirable because we will speak up for others, and some people view people like me as loudmouths or troublemakers. This speaking up can be about big things, and it can be about little things, and I think it's essential to do it especially when it could have some positive effect.

The vacation place had a tram that takes you around to different places on the grounds. We hopped on a tram that had about twelve people on it already. They all eventually got off at different stops. We came to another stop, not ours, and the driver ran into the building like he had to go to the bathroom. We sat there alone in this big empty tram for what seemed like ten minutes. Eventually an older, trim, distinguished-looking man walked out and said, "This tram doesn't have a driver, but I'll take you!" He clearly was suggesting we had boarded an empty tram. Here's where the speaking-up part comes in. I needed to let this guy know we didn't hop on an empty tram. It may have been a small thing, but if I didn't speak up then, how many more people were going to be sitting on a tram in the middle of nowhere when that tram guy left them? If he kept the job over the years, thousands. As you can see, sometimes I'm less than a barrel of laughs to hang out with.

My wife gave me a "what are you going to do now?" look. I explained I'd do it real nicely, but I had to stand up for the future tram riders, who were really in some sense my brothers and sisters—fellow tram riders, anyway. There's a kind of a communist thing right there.

We arrived at our stop. My wife and son went to hit some golf balls, and I walked over to the tram driver, who was sitting behind the wheel. I explained that we hadn't boarded an empty tram, that the driver just ran off and never came back. The man stared at me. He didn't look hostile, but his look was hard to read. I told him I thought it was good for him to hear this for overall "quality control." I actually said "quality control." He just continued to stare hard at me with virtually no readable reaction.

Soon he slowly got out of the tram to stand face-to-face with me. I started to wonder if I was heading for a fistfight. It was just a passing thought. He was about the same height as I. He looked like he spent a lot of time in a gym—not muscular but trim. Later I learned he had been one of the world's greatest athletes and had participated on the Hungarian team in the Olympics in the 1950s. Not only that, but he was a contender in the decathlon.

He continued to stare at me. I looked at him and said, very pleasantly, I assure you, "Did you hear what I was saying?" He looked at me for a moment and said, "No." There was an awkward silence, and then he said, "I was studying your face. You look so much like that man who was on Channel 38." (We were in Florida.) "His name is…his name is"—and I said, "Charles Grodin?" He said, "Yes. Charles Grodin. You resemble him so much. Are you any relation?" I said, "I am Charles Grodin." He looked at me doubtfully, suggesting my appearance didn't quite measure up to Charles Grodin standards. I muttered something about "makeup," and then he suddenly said, "Privately speaking, I love you." It was a heck of a moment.

He went on to tell me he was seventy-four years old and had been a scientist of note in Hungary. He had been imprisoned and almost killed by the Russians in the Hungarian revolution. He said, "I understand what you talk about." He then went on to suggest I had changed lately, because I seemed to be holding back the full truth sometimes, because of money, he felt. I stopped him right there and told him I hardly made any money. I actually told him I used to be in the movies where I made much more money, and money had nothing to do with what I said, which was always exactly what I thought. He nodded when I referenced the movies as though to show me he knew about that but didn't really care.

He then went on to say, "You should smile more!" I'm sure he meant on television, but he could have been referring to me right there. I was friendly, but not smiling friendly. I was thinking, Everybody's a critic! I jumped in with, "Didn't you tell me a few minutes ago you loved me?"

"Yes."

"Why don't you tell me why you love me instead of criticizing me? Why do you love me?" I was starting to feel like I was back in a scene in the movies. He said, "Because you seem to be very, very honest."

Now I smiled at him. I shook his hand and said, "Let's let it go at that," and walked away to join up with my wife and son. Altogether, it was an outstandingly positive encounter.

Two days later, I ran into him again. He walked over, shook my hand, and said, "My wife told me to tell you we will love you forever." He actually embraced me after that, and I walked away thinking if only his wife had been the tram driver it would have all been a little smoother.

Incidentally, he told me the original tram driver was a terrific young man. He didn't leave us on the tram. He was "ordered"— that was his word (this is a guy from Hungary talking)—"ordered" to have lunch. My response to that would have been so lengthy I decided at *that* moment not to speak up.

The moral of this story is to remember that whenever you choose to do that scary thing of speaking up, you have no idea where it will take you.

Speaking up has earned me a long list of adversaries. I've been attacked on television, on radio, and in most of the major publications by people who see things differently than I do.

It's a truly odd sensation to be listening to the radio and suddenly they're talking about you. I always turn it off before I can hear what they say, because I don't like to hear myself attacked when I'm not there to answer.

If I hear something negative I'll probably spend time thinking about it, and I know I can spend that time in a happier frame of mind. When there's something constructive for me to hear, I'd prefer to hear it from friends, not adversaries, and I do.

As odd as it is to suddenly hear myself attacked on radio, it's no less odd to be reading the newspaper and suddenly in the middle of an article they're attacking me. It's not like the article was about me. It's about something else that gave them an opportunity to attack me!

It doesn't feel good to have adversaries out there. It makes me feel proud, but not good.

Earlier I had sat on the co-op board of a building on Fifth Avenue in New York. There I took the position that if you could afford it, and weren't wanted by the police, I would be for letting you buy an apartment in the building.

The majority of the board members saw it differently. Sometimes it felt as if they were truly reaching to come up with a reason to keep a buyer out. I can only assume they figured the more exclusive they were, the more expensive the apartments would be. Maybe that's not true, but why would you say as a critical comment about a potential buyer, "He gets his clothes off the rack"? I said, "I get *my* clothes off the rack." They said, "We know."

They'd seriously question whether an applicant's personal references were really friends or actually business associates. It wouldn't be great if you came from the garment center. They had a million of them.

I spoke up over and over there, but given the prevailing elitist point of view, I became more of a curiosity than a serious protestor. So I kept a lot of notes and, trying to make chicken salad out of chicken s—, I wrote a play about it.

Locally, in youth sports, I've been speaking up for years. So much so that recently a Little League manager came over to me and said, "I hope you don't mind, but I had to put a parent's name on the protest committee, and I put you down."

I asked, "Protest regarding what?" He said, "We don't have any protests at this time, but if we do I'd like you to be the parent protestor."

The last time I spoke up or protested locally had to do with a situation involving a boy who had been on the basketball and football teams from the fifth through the seventh grade. The boy broke his arm playing football on the team in the eighth grade. He was unable to try out for the eighth-grade basketball team, as his arm was in a cast.

Even though he would recover and be able to play shortly after the basketball season began, he was ruled ineligible, as he wasn't available to try out.

The eighth-grade basketball coach, a supermentor named Blake Billmire, called to make me aware of the situation. I got in touch with a couple of my associates who had sat on the basketball oversight committee with me and arranged a hearing. The coach and the people at the Parks and Recreation Department who were in charge of the program and who were enforcing the rules, along with the elected officials from the town who had the final say, were all there.

Parks and Rec's position was that, in the past, players who had established themselves on the team sometimes just blew off the tryouts, saying they were unavailable for one reason or another, knowing they'd later be on the team. That's why Parks and Rec felt if you couldn't make one of the two tryouts, you shouldn't be on the squad. Nowhere in the rules was there anything dealing with an authentic injury making a player unavailable for the tryout.

It seemed like a no-brainer to me. How could you possibly keep a kid off the basketball team who was as hard-playing a young athlete as anyone in the town, a boy who had broken his arm playing football for the town, and not only that but by sheer grit had worked his way up to become one of the stars of the basketball team?

The other side argued that we wanted him there precisely because he was such a good player, and we wouldn't be bothering to protest the rule if he was a backup player.

That was absolutely not true. I would have taken the same position for anyone on the team who'd gotten injured prior to tryouts. I'd also be for holding a special tryout for anyone who was unavailable to try out because of injury, whether they had been on the team or not.

Even though I'd been on the basketball oversight committee for years, I'd never heard of this rule that eliminated the kid.

The other side was saying that a rule was a rule, and as the meeting came to an end I felt the rule would be changed, but prior to next season, not now.

I drove to work feeling I had failed the boy. As the elected officials were meeting to give their decision, I quickly faxed them a letter. I said I felt they would eventually change the rule, but asked them to please consider doing it right now, so such a deserving young athlete wouldn't be punished.

The next day the coach called to say the boy would be allowed to play. It was enormously gratifying to me.

Sometimes everywhere things are obviously so wrong, and un-accountably they're *not* changed.

The boy went on to have a wonderful season, and, of course, the people on the other side were more than a little annoyed with me.

Speaking up is no picnic. I'd rather just be a quiet, thoughtful type of guy—if I had a choice.

Back to Television—
60 Minutes II

Jeff Fager came to my house to hear more pieces that I had prepared for him for *60 Minutes II.* By this time, I'd actually had a birthday. I later learned that Jeff is this thorough about everything, and it shows in what he produces. He came at my suggestion, as I found it increasingly awkward to go to his office. Jeff lives in a town near mine, so it was easy for him to come by. I debated where to work with Jeff. This was actually the first time I'd had a business meeting at my house. I've never been interviewed there either, but this seemed right, under the circumstances. I have a study where I work with a lot of framed photos, awards, etc. If I wanted someone to be aware of all my achievements, which I certainly wanted Jeff to be, that would be the place to hold the session. On the other hand, it's like sitting surrounded by an ad for myself, so I picked a room that had no awards for me.

Although Jeff Fager appears to be very relaxed and easygoing, he can quickly transition to a surprising intensity. While he was again very receptive to what I read him, his critical comments were as sharp as I'd ever heard.

Jeff stayed for two hours and then asked if he could see any place in the house we might later choose to tape. Even though it was highly unlikely, for invasion-of-the-house-by-a-television-crew reasons, I took the opportunity to show him the earlier ruled-out study. It's a spacious room with a view of wooded hillsides, which Jeff appreciated, and, of course, he couldn't help but notice a few awards.

While in my study Jeff told me he was on a flight recently with Dan Rather, who had suggested me for this job.

Of course, I was very pleased. Dan Rather, among his other responsibilities, is a correspondent for *60 Minutes II.*

We made plans for me to come to New York the following week to do some more pieces, which Jeff would then show to the people who had to sign off on this.

It was April. If all went well, I knew I could begin this marvelous job in August, one that felt more right than anything I could have imagined.

Once again I drove to New York for what would be the last test. I knew Jeff liked the pieces I was going to do, as he chose them from a larger group.

I believed what we were doing was exploring the way to present this material. This is, of course, a form unto itself, where Andy Rooney is the master. (I had met Andy once a few years earlier. We shook hands. I said hello. He said, "You have a strange, unusual style." Jokingly I said, "You could tell that just from hello?" Later I walked alone with him to his car and we had some laughs.) Doing commentary for *60 Minutes II* was not like anything I'd done before. On my show in the monologue, there was no script. Here, there was. It wasn't like acting, which I've done for so long. This was its own special form, and Jeff had very definite feelings about it.

I arrived around 9:30 in the morning as the crew was setting up in the hotel suite. Jeff arrived around two hours later. The moment we began, it was clear he was pleased. At the end he seemed very happy, and so, of course, was I. I drove home more optimistic than ever. The next step would be for Jeff to show his selections to a couple of people at the top of CBS.

Finally, after six months, I got the call I'd been waiting for. Jeff Fager phoned and offered me the job. I had been led to believe this was going to happen for so long that the call was kind of anticlimactic. Looking back, I think the biggest charge was when Jeff handed me the *60 Minutes II* pen!

In the call I again asked Jeff his feeling about my doing movies, and this time he felt I shouldn't.

I agreed with him. I'm always a little thrown when I see Senator Fred Thompson from Tennessee in the movies or on television playing a character similar to himself. He hasn't done this lately, since he's actually been elected to the Senate, but because of all the reruns, it feels as though he has. Even though I find Fred Thompson more straightforward than most politicians, as a group they always seem to be acting a little anyway. So to have public figures actually appearing as actors, well... the whole concept makes me a little dizzy.

Ronald Reagan once said he couldn't imagine being president without having been an actor.

People assume the connection is that politicians and actors both pretend in their professions, that they are both reading scripts. Of course, there's truth in that, but for me the most significant advantage a politician has if he's been an actor is that he's used to appearing in public in front of large groups of people.

When's the last time you appeared in public in front of a large group of people? Don't try this, or, if you want to appear in front of large groups of people, start with small groups, like with two friends.

The first time you get up in front of a large group of people to speak, you'll really wish you hadn't. The trick is to forget about how many people are watching and just focus on what you have to say. Actors know this, and if they later become politicians they put it to use. If you're really relaxed in front of a large crowd, almost no matter what you stand for, you could get elected to something.

In thinking about Jeff Fager, I realized who he reminded me of. One of my favorite people I've ever worked with is the film director Mike Nichols. Jeff, like Mike, is extremely bright. Jeff, like Mike, has enormous enthusiasms. Jeff, like Mike, is able to criticize in a positive manner, not by tearing down but by suggesting something better.

He's always raising the bar, but because he's so supportive and enthusiastic, you have the will to reach higher. It strikes me as a good lesson in parenting as well as producing.

I look back on the whole saga of my television experience, and I know if at any time someone had asked me what I would consider my ideal job in television, I would have answered, "Something like what Andy Rooney does on *60 Minutes.*"

When I was a teenager, I was heading to the University of Pittsburgh to be a journalism major. Shortly after actually being "rushed" by fraternities there, I saw the movie *A Place in the Sun* and decided I wanted to become an actor like Montgomery Clift and hopefully one day meet Elizabeth Taylor. (I did, too, and we were both single, but nothing happened.)

In my thirty-year career in the movies I found myself from time to time being pulled back toward my original intention of journalism. It manifested in the sixties with the Simon and Garfunkel special, in the seventies with Carol Burnett and the Friendly movement, and in the eighties with books and magazine articles. In the nineties came my cable show, which evolved from "dessert" to advocacy, and in the year 2000 I joined *60 Minutes II*. It's been quite a winding road, but I feel as though I'm finally where I was meant to be. From the movies to CNBC to MSNBC to *60 Minutes II*, what a ride this has been.

Epilogue

I've now completed my first year on *60 Minutes II,* and when people ask me how I like it, I try very hard to avoid sounding like the clichéd talk show guest I never wanted to be, but it *is* a wonderful experience and I *am* very grateful for the opportunity.

I've received much appreciated support and approval from the public as well as the people at the broadcast, and no one has been more supportive than Andy Rooney.

Shortly after beginning on the show, I gave a Christmas party at my house, and Andy came. I told him about a negative e-mail that had gotten through that ripped me just about every way imaginable. It ended by saying, "You'll never be another Andy Rooney." Andy immediately jumped in with, "Well, I've been watching you. I think you've got it made. You're really good."

Coming from him, you can imagine what that meant to me. Another time he called me the morning after a broadcast and left a message saying, "I thought you'd be home accepting congratulations, and I wanted to add my name to the list." Throughout the whole season, I called on him for advice on different issues, and he was always available, warm, and invaluable, as he was speaking to me from his unique perspective.

When my wife and I had dinner with Andy and his wife and a friend, at the end of the evening he said softly to me, "Well, this was good. It gives us a chance to get to know each other." He was so gracious and modest.

I told Andy that I had some confusion about how to conduct myself as a member of CBS News, and I thought it would be helpful to read a transcript of an appearance he had made with Larry King, where I knew Larry and the callers would ask him every imaginable question.

In that interview Andy was against everything from the World War II monument to the overused concept of heroes to saying that any generation was the greatest. Earlier he had come out against making Halloween costumes, tanks, and saying "God bless America." You never have to wonder what Andy Rooney really thinks. Agree with him or not, he's a treasure. I'm sure he's against referring to people as treasures too, but just this once.

From what has filtered through of the nature of the complaints about me, they seem much less to be on the content of the commentary than on me personally. "How can you hire such a big liberal?"

Again, I don't think it's liberal to say we need to talk much more about the disadvantaged people in our country. I have no idea what the solutions are, whether they're Liberal or Conservative or Independent, or Green Party or Libertarian or any other. I'm just saying we have to put those in need front and center of our focus. The first job of government is to provide security, the second, to look after the needy, then everything else.

People listen to that and I know think to themselves, He *is* a big liberal.

"No child should be left behind" is a sentiment often expressed by politicians of both parties. It's not a liberal or a conservative concept. It's a human one. Of course, children—and adults—have always been left behind. We have millions of children who have inadequate schooling, inadequate housing, and no health insurance, who go to bed hungry and, of course, will not be prepared for good jobs. We even have large numbers of mentally ill children being held in prisons.

It is really indulgent to talk about party labels in dealing with these overwhelming problems. Everyone's focus should be on solutions, not name-calling.

When I came to New York, I could only afford a tiny room without a window and a bathroom down the hall in a seedy hotel. It cost ten dollars a week. I had seen a room in someone's large apartment that had a beautiful view of the Hudson River. It was a dollar a week more. It was a vastly more desirable living situation for me. The problem was that they wanted a couple of months' rent in advance, and I didn't have it. I didn't want to ask my mother or my brother for it. I got a job that paid me a dollar an hour, and I never got money from home, so obviously I don't believe in a free lunch.

I guess what separates me from some others is that I don't see us as all having the same opportunity and therefore capability. I had two parents at home and a remarkable older brother. There weren't drugs and crime outside my door and cockroaches and rats in the house.

The schools were good and safe, and the whole environment

when I was growing up was way better than it is today for millions of kids. When conditions are crushing, it's easier to lose hope than some people seem to understand.

Of course, everyone should work, but if you're not qualified for anything that could pay your bills, the powers that be should do everything possible to help you get qualified.

To use a favorite quote, "If we're not for ourselves, then who will be, but if we're only for ourselves, what are we?"

The biggest thing that's happened in these recent months was that three more people for whose clemency I worked received it.

I am one of a long list of people who worked on behalf of Leah Bundy, Donna Charles, and Terence Stevens. Leah Bundy was one of the four women I originally sought clemency for, and few people thought she would get it. There really is a difference between being tough on crime and being cruel, and happily some people in power know it.

People often come up to me and ask if I'm going to be doing any more movies, or they'll say they miss seeing me on my cable show, and of course I appreciate all of it. I, too, have missed my cable show, and the freedom to say anything anytime without an approved script that only cable or radio seems to allow.

I have to say, though, with twelve million viewers a week for *60 Minutes II* in America alone, along with countless millions in countries all over the world, this opportunity to do commentary is remarkable. While Jeff Fager has to approve what I've written, our disagreements are about whether he believes my commentary is compelling enough for the broadcast, never about my right to express what I believe. Happily, he accepts most of what I offer with enthusiasm.

I particularly had fun with an early piece I did on the sponsorship of the most unlikely elements of a baseball game.

The picnic area was sponsored by Pepsi. The umpires as well as the call to the bullpen were sponsored. The starting lineup, the schedule, and even the scoreboard were sponsored, and, of course, more and more stadiums themselves have sponsors' names.

A couple in the news recently tried to sell naming rights for their newborn to a sponsor, but I don't think anyone bit.

The companies, of course, are looking for the celebrity tie-ins. I did a piece on that when *McCall's* magazine became *Rosie's McCall's*, with Rosie O'Donnell on the cover just as Martha Stewart and Oprah have their own magazines. We used to have Arnold Palmer golf clubs, but now Arnold's associated with a tire company.

When two top experts on diets came out for and against the same things, I did a piece on that. Dr. Dean Ornish told us to avoid all meats. Dr. Robert Atkins told us to eat all meats. Dr. Ornish wants us to eat legumes, grains, and fruits. Dr. Atkins wants us to avoid grains and fruits. He doesn't say anything about legumes.

I've also been able to say to all these millions of people that I believe hitting children under any circumstances is wrong. I know there are many who disagree, and I've heard the arguments on the other side, but hitting of any kind teaches that violence is a way to settle problems. You spank a kid who may hit his kid harder than you hit him, and on and on, leading inevitably in some cases to real violence. In the long run, it's really not a good idea.

I've been able to reach millions of people to add my voice to those who warn that all these distractions that are going into cars are dangerous. I'm talking about, in addition to phones, fax machines, and even e-mail. In cars!

Maybe the commentary I did in my first season that got the most attention was built around my trip to the New York Mets baseball facility in Port St. Lucie, Florida, during spring training for the 2001 season.

The piece featured a strategy session with manager Bobby Valentine as well as my giving a pep talk to star slugger Mike Piazza. The Mets had been to the World Series the season before, and in the commentary I expressed my hope that my advice might not only get them back to the World Series but help them win it.

The Mets went on to have one of their worst seasons in years.

Look, you do what you can and hope for the best.

Postscript: September 11

I'm writing this about two months after the attack on the World Trade Center and the Pentagon.

On the morning of September 11, I was listening to the radio while getting ready to drive into New York City to hear the first reading of a play I had written. Later I planned to go to CBS to do some work over there.

Like most people when the news came that a plane had hit the World Trade Center, I assumed it was an accident. I went to the television and saw the second plane hit, but again, like many others, even after I saw it with my own eyes it was hard to comprehend the enormity of what was actually happening. Sometimes our minds work in strange ways.

To the dismay of my wife, I decided to head into New York City to keep my appointments. I live about an hour north, and as I entered the parkway, the traffic seemed normal. After a little while, as I heard of the attack on the Pentagon on the radio, I noticed that the traffic heading into the city began to thin. After about forty minutes, more and more cars turned off at exits on the parkway. I kept going, as I felt no personal sense of danger.

As I got closer to Manhattan, my car was the only one on the parkway heading in that direction. Phones were out all over the city, so I couldn't reach anyone at the theater where the play was to be read, nor could I reach my producer at CBS.

Eventually I saw a state trooper standing in the middle of the highway with his hands raised, indicating that I should stop. "National emergency, sir," he said, and he waved me toward a nearby exit that would allow me to turn around and head back north, which I did.

About two weeks later, I went to ground zero, this time in a police car with my *60 Minutes II* producer, Chris Martin. I didn't want to take a film crew with me. There were plenty of reporters taking care of that, including, of course, the journalists from our broadcast. It felt appropriate that I go, since I knew I'd be talking about this not only on *60 Minutes II* but for the CBS News Radio network, for which I was now also doing commentaries.

A few miles north of the site, life seemed absolutely normal. People were walking their dogs. I even saw kids playing in a sandbox. If you didn't know where it was coming from, you wouldn't have given a second thought to the touch of smoke in the air.

As the police car approached about a mile from ground zero, it all changed. There were barricades everywhere. The only people walking through were police officers and people who could prove they lived in the area.

Even the uniformed officer driving the police car I was in had to show identification.

At some point we got out of the car and began to walk toward what looked like the widest, biggest pile of rubble I've ever seen. The blackened buildings left standing on the perimeter of the devastation, of course, had their windows shattered. At one point the police officer pointed to a mass of rubble and said, "That was the Marriott hotel."

Later that night, my son asked me where all the bodies were that our police and firefighters were looking for. "Are they down deep?" he wondered. As he spoke, he looked away from me. I looked away from him as I answered, "Most of them probably don't exist."

It was only at that moment that I realized I had just visited a monstrous burial site.

As everyone knows, this was the biggest attack on America since the Japanese bombed Pearl Harbor in 1941. I remember as a six-year-old standing at the top of the steps that led to our basement and asking my brother, who was twelve, if the Japanese were coming to Pittsburgh. "Yes, they are," he said. I said, "Well, they won't come to our house, will they?" He said, "Yes, they will." I then said, "Well, I'm going down into the basement. They won't come down there, will they?" "Yes, they will," he answered. Ironically, this time we were hoping the enemy *would* show up somewhere.

On radio and television I began to talk about airline security.

Over the years, I had done a number of programs on this subject on my cable show. My most knowledgeable guest was Mary Schiavo, the former inspector general of the Department of Transportation who had been the biggest critic of the airlines and their supervisory agency, the Federal Aviation Administration.

In 1991, Mary had testified before Congress about insufficient airport security and poorly trained personnel. She pointed out that the FAA foolishly had the dual task of monitoring the airlines and supporting them.

Nothing seemed to change over the years. There were remarkable breaches of security, which continue at this writing, two months after the attack.

One expert who tested the system for a long period said he got through more than 90 percent of the time—with weapons! Dynamite and hand grenades have gotten through. Government agents have even gotten through with four fake bombs! The list of serious security breaches is endless.

Speaking after the attack, Jane Garvey, an FAA administrator, asked, "Who could have imagined such a thing?" That remark astonished me. Surely someone responsible for our security must know that in World War II the Japanese flew their planes into our warships. Over the years we've seen a number of hijackings. We know that there are terrorists willing to blow themselves up. If you work in security, how hard is it to put all of that into one picture? The phrase *criminal negligence* keeps coming to mind.

United Airlines responded to all of this in a strange way. They ran commercials featuring a pilot literally saying, "When I say hello, I really mean it." As though the reason people were fearful of flying was that they questioned the captain's sincerity!

After September 11, Don Imus seemed to drop much of his general venom and conducted outstanding interviews with newsmakers. After a few weeks, his full hostility returned. Sometimes he seems to be suffering from a form of Tourette's syndrome. Then one day he admitted on the air that every time he heard there were civilian casualties in Afghanistan he wished the number were higher. Just when you thought you'd heard everything! I guess there are no limits to some people's detachment.

As I've said, I can't look at Bill O'Reilly's smug, self-righteous face on his show, but I did watch him for about a minute as he was being interviewed by Tim Russert on Tim's weekend cable show.

Predictably, he wore his rage over September 11 as a badge of honor. Obviously we're all enraged, but O'Reilly needs to be the most enraged. This would all resonate a little better if he hadn't been enraged for years. In the past it was against network executives. Now he's in a lawsuit with his next-door neighbor. I don't doubt Mr. O'Reilly's rage over September 11. I also believe he has a general problem with rage.

Commercials about depression began to spring up all over radio and television. One day while I was in my car I heard one about something called major depressive disorder. It asked something like "Are you feeling down, kind of anxious, not sleeping as well as you'd like, seem to have lost that get-up-and-go? Well, you may be suffering from major depressive disorder. If you'd like to be a member of a group for study, call 1-800-so-and-so." I thought, You may not be suffering from major depressive disorder—that might just mean you're alive.

Corporations started to refer to the attack in their commercials, and sometimes it seemed a bit much. One guy came on the radio and in a very deep voice said something like "Whatever is going on today, there's always hope for tomorrow. Tomorrow is a time of renewal when we can begin anew." There was a lot of other stuff I can't really remember about hope and tomorrow. It turned out to be a commercial for the New York lottery.

About six weeks later, I went to Reading, Pennsylvania, for a personal appearance.

I told the audience about something my son had read me from "Ripley's Believe It or Not!" According to Ripley, in 1939 a man named George Stofflit from Reading was hit on the head by a cooked trout that fell out of the sky, I assume from a plane.

I said that this was the first time I had been out of the New York area since September 11, and it definitely seemed more relaxed in Amish country. However...I then looked up at the ceiling to make sure no cooked trout was going to hit me in the head. Thanks to Ripley, we all had a good laugh.

Acknowledgments

I wish to thank my editor, Jonathan Karp, for his enthusiasm, sensitivity, and high intelligence.

I'd like to thank my representative, Owen Laster, for his confidence in me and his appreciation of whatever it is I do.

I'd like to thank my television representative, Jimmy Griffin, who's always standing in the wings, ready to catch me.

I'd like to thank my typist, Rose Snyder. This is my fifth book, and I still write longhand, but if I didn't, I never would have met Rose.

I'd like to thank Janelle Duryea, Steve Messina, Sally Marvin, Carol Schneider, Kapo Ng, and Andy Carpenter of Random House for their support and goodwill.

I'd like to thank my wife, Elissa, my daughter, Marion, and my son, Nick. They seem to like what I do, and that really helps me do it.

Index

Numbers in italics refer to photographs.

About the Author

CHARLES GRODIN has had a unique career path, from Broadway to Hollywood to television commentary. Along the way he has written four acclaimed books, including *It Would Be So Nice If You Weren't Here,* which was a national bestseller. Mr. Grodin won an Outer Critics Circle Award as best actor in *Same Time, Next Year* on Broadway. He won an Emmy Award as a writer for *The Paul Simon Special.* For thirty years he starred in a number of outstanding films, including *The Heartbreak Kid, Seems Like Old Times, Midnight Run,* and the *Beethoven* movies. In 1995 Mr. Grodin began a successful career as a television talk show host; he received four Cable Ace Award nominations for *The Charles Grodin Show,* which appeared on CNBC and MSNBC. He is currently the commentator for the CBS newsmagazine program *60 Minutes II* as well as a commentator for the CBS News Radio network. He has written for *The New York Times*, *Esquire*, and *The Village Voice*, among other publications. He lives in Connecticut with his wife and son.

About the Type

The text of this book was set in Janson, a misnamed typeface designed in about 1690 by Nicholas Kis, a Hungarian in Amsterdam. In 1919 the matrices became the property of the Stempel Foundry in Frankfurt. It is an old-style book face of excellent clarity and sharpness. Janson serifs are concave and splayed; the contrast between thick and thin strokes is marked.